T0197139

MY
FATHER'S
NAME

CHARLES P. EVERETT, IV

authorHOUSE

AuthorHouse™
1663 Liberty Drive
Bloomington, IN 47403
www.authorhouse.com
Phone: 833-262-8899

Published by AuthorHouse 02/24/2023

ISBN: 978-1-6655-7443-3 (sc)
ISBN: 978-1-6655-7444-0 (hc)
ISBN: 978-1-6655-7555-3 (e)

Library of Congress Control Number: 2022919904

CONTENTS

ACKNOWLEDGEMENTS

When God created moral men and women, He desired for them to be fruitful and multiply. Our family has followed that moral directive as evidenced by our family tree. The family of Charles P. and Alfredia B. Everett came into existence because of the shared relationships of many ancestors and by the grace of God. This book is written in their memory. It has also been developed so that this generation and all future generations may be able to learn about those who made countless sacrifices so that we have been able to participate in an evolving process of life, liberty and the pursuit of happiness.

INTRODUCTION

My father, Charles Patterson Everett, Sr., was greatly influenced by a flawed practice he had inherited from his father and grandfather. That custom was founded on the belief that in the Everett family, the paternal grandfather never lived to see the birth of his grandson. That had certainly been the case with him and his grandfather and me and mine for they had died before we were born. However, that did not prove true for Daddy and his grandsons and me and my grandsons. This belief had led to the practice of the older living Charles inheriting the suffix Senior (Sr.) and the next in lineage, Junior (Jr.). This custom had led to a record-keeping nightmare for the Alabama State Department of Education where my grandfather's, father's and my professional records were identified under the name Charles P. Everett, Jr. It became my responsibility to straighten out the confusion by assigning each Charles his proper suffix. As I participated in this exercise, not only did I discover the NAME to be a conundrum, but I also learned that it would become the source from which the history of the paternal side of my family would flow.

CHAPTER 1

SEARCH FOR THE PATRIARCH

As STATED EARLIER, TRACING THE HISTORY OF MY FATHER'S NAME HAS been difficult; however, a bit of information provided by my cousin, Eugene Jarrett has made it possible to locate invaluable facts about the origin of the Everett family. In 1977, he told my father that Charles Everett, his grandfather had fought in the Civil War and was buried in Arlington National Cemetery. Upon learning of this, my father called me and reported the startling revelation.

I immediately made a long-distance call to the Superintendent of Graves at Arlington and asked him if a Charles Everett was listed among those buried there. After checking his records, he indicated that he was not. Undaunted by his reply, I continued my search. This had been the closest I had gotten to learning more about my paternal great-grandfather.

My wife Alfredia and I had traveled to Hampton, Virginia a few years earlier in search of facts about my grandfather who had matriculated at Hampton Institute. While there, I had visited the campus of Hampton Institute now University. There, the oldest African American museum in the United States of America is housed. Located near the campus was a military cemetery. Could this have been the place to which Eugene had referred? With this thought in mind, I contacted the Superintendent of Graves at the Hampton National Military Cemetery. Eureka! The patriarch of the Everett family had been interred there in 1909.

It would not be until August of 1998 that I would be able to visit the grave and take photographs. On a sultry summer afternoon, Alfredia and I drove our Chevy Blazer through the gated entrance of the cemetery. Lying ahead of us were thousands of white headstones standing proudly like silent sentinels over the graves of our nation's heroes. Upon getting out of our vehicle and walking through the area, we were able to locate my great-grandfather's grave. On the tombstone, the following inscription was displayed: 9742 SE2CT. CHAS. EVERETT USCT.

From where had Charles come? What was the origin of his name? Who were his parents? Where had they lived? Some of the answers to these questions would be found in his military records which had been housed in the National Archives in Washington D.C.

In his military records, he indicated that he was enslaved from birth, and did not know who his parents were. He reported two individuals who had enslaved him. They were Isaac Patterson and John Everett of Caswell County, North Carolina. The enlistment documents do not indicate the chronological order of his enslavement. In the name that he chose to call himself, he listed Patterson as the middle name and Everett as the surname. The report also declares that Charles was born in Caswell County.

That location was named for Richard Caswell who was born in 1729 and died in 1789. He was a member of the First Continental Congress. He was also the first governor of North Carolina after America was declared independent of England.

It is interesting to note at this juncture that one of the foundational statements in the Declaration of Independence declares: "We hold these truths to be self-evident that all men are created equal, that they are endowed by their Creator with certain unalienable Rights that among these are Life, Liberty and the pursuit of Happiness." This statement has been so imperfectly applied in the evolution of my family. Although the statement declares that all men are created equal, my family has not been treated equally. Our journey reflects a nation that is becoming a more perfect union too slowly. Charles, the enslaved human being was not considered a whole man but only three fifths and was not allowed to enjoy "these truths" declared in the sentence. The word unalienable refers to those rights that could not be given away or taken away; however, black men and black and white women were not included. John Everett and Isaac Patterson were allowed, by law to take those rights away from Charles.

Caswell County was also where Kizzy, the great-great-great grandmother of Alex Haley, the author of <u>Roots</u>, was enslaved.[1] Kizzy had been sold to Tom Moore, a planter who owned property there. It was on that plantation that Moore raped Kizzy which resulted in their giving birth to a baby who was named George. George grew up

---

[1] Haley, Alex. <u>Roots.</u> Garden City, N.Y.: Doubleday, 1976. Print.

to become a competitive cock fighter who was nicknamed "Chicken George." His family would remain in North Carolina until after the Civil War when they would move to Tennessee.

Both Isaac Patterson and John Everett are listed in the Census of 1850. In that document, Isaac Patterson is a white farmer who lived in Surry, North Carolina. He was born in 1792. Residing with him were Nancy his wife aged 40, and his children William-19, Turner-15, Mary A.-14, Pelina-13, and Martha-8. Isaac's name is also listed in the census reports of 1830 and 1840.

The report for John Everett indicates he was born in 1767. The 83-year-old man had no spouse listed, and he did not have children; however, the following individuals lived in his home in Caswell County, North Carolina: Elisha Slaton-28, Martha M. Slaton-25, and their children Daniel-1, William-3, and Eliza F.-2. He died on June 20, 1858.

In his will dated May 27, 1858, and executed in July of 1858, he made the following pronouncement: "My estate both real and personal I wish to be sold and the money equally divided between my brothers' and sisters' children. I wish my rent to be collected and the money divided between my brothers' and sisters' children. My will and desire is that my Negroes shall have the privilege of selecting their masters, their value to be ascertained by two disinterested men one selected by the master they choose and one by my executor. I appointment my friends Samuel Harrison, Joseph S. Totten and Daniel Everett Executors to this my last will and testament. I do hereby revoke and declare utterly void all other wills and testaments by me heretofore made in witness whereof I the said John Everett do hereunto fix my hand and seal, this the 27th of May 1858."[2] The witnesses were a Mr. Slade and John Chandler. Since John Everett could not write, he affixed his mark, an "x" to the will. In the will he also gave four slaves to his nephew Daniel Everett and two Negro girls to Agnes Ferguson.

In November of 1858, the executors of the estate sought clarification of the clause in the will permitting John's slaves to choose their own masters. The executors believed it was doubtful whether a "slave can

---

[2] Caswell County Will Books 1843-1868.

select his master or do any act requiring judgment and will."[3] The North Carolina Supreme Court rejected the petition.

How and when Charles escaped bondage to Isaac Patterson or John Everett remains a mystery to me. Enshrined in that mystery, however, was the hope that the rumors swirling through the community about emancipation would come true and be a step toward his being given his life, liberty, and pursuit of happiness. Enslaved people in Caswell County, were being told that if they would escape to the Union lines, there would be an opportunity to fight for their freedom. Charles would rather die fighting for his freedom than remain in subjugation to another human being.

The roots of the rumors were grounded in truth. It was a fact that on September 22, 1862, President Abraham Lincoln signed an executive order which became known as the Emancipation Proclamation. It declared that as of January 1, 1863, "all persons held as slaves within any State or designated part of a State, the people whereof shall then be in rebellion against the United States, shall be then, thenceforward, and forever free; and the Executive Government of the United States, including the military and naval authority thereof, will recognize and maintain the freedom of such persons, and will do no act or acts to repress such persons, or any of them, in any efforts they may make for their actual freedom."[4]

On June 8, 1863, Charles joined the Union Army and was assigned to Company C, First Regiment of the United States Colored Infantry at Washington D. C. He was enlisted by Colonial Birney for a term of three years. On his enrollment form, J. A. Wise the copyist described him as being thirty-three years of age. His height was five feet nine inches. His complexion was very swarthy, and he had a scar on the right side of his upper lip. His eyes and hair were black.

---

[3] Order - November Term 1858; Reports of Cases in Equity, Supreme Court of North Carolina, December 1859-August 1860, pp.163-164.

[4] Emancipation Proclamation, January 1, 1863; Presidential Proclamations, 1791-1991; Record Group 11; General Records of the United States Government; National Archives.

First U. S. Colored Infantry
Mathew Brady – Photographer (Courtesy Library of Congress)

His military records indicate two indisputable facts: one, that he served as a recruiter, and two, his infantry took part in combat. It participated in the following military activities during his tour of duty:

Explosion of mines at Petersburg – July 30, 1863;
Siege of Petersburg – July, 1863;
Demonstration on the north side of the James River –
    September 28-30, 1863;
The Battle of Chaffin's Farm, New Market Heights –
    September 28-30. 1863;
The Battle of Fair Oaks – October 27-28, 1863;
Expedition to Fort Fisher, N. C. – December 7-27, 1863;
Second expedition to Fort Fisher, N. C. – January 7-15, 1865
Assault on and capture of Fort Fisher – January 15, 1865;
The Battle of Sugar Loaf Hill – January 19, 1865;
Capture of Wilmington – February 22, 1865;
Campaign of the Carolinas – March 1-April 26, 1865;
Advance on Goldsboro – March 6-21, 1865;

Advance on Raleigh – April 9-13, 1865;
Occupation of Raleigh – April 13, 1865;
Surrender of Johnston and his Army – April 1865.

In the year 1864, Charles was also actively engaged. From May to June, he was one of one thousand-eight-hundred black men who repulsed the cavalry division of Major General Fitzhugh Lee at the Battle of Wilson's Wharf in Charles City, Virginia. There were about three thousand men in Lee's cavalry division which attacked the Union supply depot at Wilson's Wharf. Under the leadership of Brigadier General Edward Wild two black regiments won a victory for the Union. One hundred sixty-five soldiers died in that battle.

On June 15-18, 1864, Corporal Everett participated in the Battle of Petersburg in Virginia. The Union army was under the leadership of General Ulysses Grant and Major General George Meade. The principal commanders for the Confederacy were General Robert E. Lee and General P. G. T. Beauregard, who provided enough Confederate reinforcements to defend Petersburg adequately. Sixty-two thousand Union soldiers engaged forty-two thousand Confederate soldiers. There were eleven thousand three hundred eighty-six casualties (8,150 Union and 3,236 Confederate). The Union army was victorious at Petersburg.

The victory at Petersburg was so important because it meant the disruption of a crucial supply route of five separate railroads that transported crucial supplies from the south to Richmond, Virginia, and other Confederate strongholds. This victory ultimately led to Lee's surrender and the beginning of the end of the American Civil War.

Sargent Charles Patterson Everett's military career came to an end on September 29, 1865, when he was discharged at Roanoke Island, North Carolina. From his enlistment to January 1, 1864, he was paid a salary of ten dollars a month from which three dollars was deducted for clothing. The remaining seven dollars is equivalent to one hundred eighty dollars and seventy-one cents in 2022 U. S. currency. White soldiers were paid three dollars more per month. He was promoted from corporal to sergeant on June 30, 1864.

On June 19, 1865, just before his discharge, he was married at Roanoke Island to Mary Ann Wiggins. Reverend William O. Turner, who later became a bishop in Georgia, performed the marriage ceremony. That year he went to work as a farmer in Danville, Virginia. According to the Census Report of 1870, he and Mary lived in a home on Butts Road in Norfolk, Virginia. He was forty years old, and Mary was eighteen. At that time, the couple had given birth to two children: Nancy born in 1866, and Louisa born in 1868.

By the 1880 census, Charles was a farm laborer and Mary was a housekeeper. Three more children had been born: Charles P., Jr. – 1870, Mary A. – 1873, and John – 1874. They were still living in Norfolk. That year, the couple experienced a marital separation. Mary left Charles in Norfolk, and she returned to North Carolina with her five children. By the time of the separation, Charles, Sr. had become a log rafter. He and Mary did not correspond with one another during their separation.

Sometime later, however, Mary had received word that Charles was knocked off a raft of logs and drowned. Charles who had remained in Norfolk, contacted a friend who had just returned from North Carolina a few weeks prior to their meeting. This individual told him that Mary had died.

Believing that Mary was deceased, Charles married Cherry Sumner on October 12, 1883. W. N. Newbold who may have been a Justice of the Peace for Perquimans County, North Carolina, applied for their marriage license. On the marriage license neither listed the names of their parents which was typical of those born into slavery, nor did Cherry know her birth year. Their marriage would last for eleven years.

In 1893, something most unexpected occurred. While walking down a street in Norfolk one day, Charles met his first wife Mary whom up to that point he had believed dead. After the shocking reunion, Mary and Charles continued to communicate with each other; however, they continued to live separately; he with Cherry and she with her daughter Mary Ballard and her husband in Hampton, Virginia.

In 1894, Charles caught Cherry in an adulterous relationship with an individual named George Bradshaw. This caused him to leave

Cherry, taking his property with him from the house where he had lived in Phoebus, Virginia. After separating from her, he consulted a lawyer who told him that since Mary, the mother of his children, was still living, not being dead as he had thought at the time of his marriage to Cherry Sumner that he had a right and a duty to return to his legal wife. This he immediately did. Soon after, they began to live on New Road in the Chesapeake District.

Cherry claiming to be his wife sued out a warrant before S. O. Houchens who was then a duly qualified Justice of the Peace for Elizabeth City County, Virginia, charging Charles with bigamy for having married her while Mary was still living. This led to Charles being arrested and examined by H. O. Houchens. During the trial, Cherry was present. They and other witnesses were given an opportunity to testify. After a thorough examination, Charles was discharged. The Justice of the Peace found him not guilty. During that year, 1899, Mary died.

During his final years of earthly life, Sgt. Charles P. Everett, Sr. was a resident of the Southern Branch of the National Home for Disabled Volunteer Soldiers. This facility was designed as an integrated facility for military veterans. The campus is located at 100 Emancipation Drive in Hampton, Virginia. This means that Charles P. Everett, Sr. was the first member of our family known to live in an integrated governmental institution. According to pension certificate number 454452, Charles P. Everett, Sr. died there on June 2, 1909. His death preceded my father's birth.

Photograph of Veterans at the Southern Branch of the
National Home for Disabled Veterans in Hampton,
Virginia (Courtesy of the Library of Congress)

CHAPTER 2

CHARLES P. EVERETT, JR.

THE 1890S WERE VERY EVENTFUL FOR THE EVERETT FAMILY. NOT only had there been domestic turbulence in the family, but there was also joy. On September 23, 1890, Charles P. Everett, Jr. entered Hampton Normal and Agricultural Institute, becoming the first member of our family to accomplish such a noble act. He matriculated there from 1890 to 1895 when he completed the course of study. The son of a formerly enslaved father who never learned to read or write, Charles, Jr. had accomplished what was thought to be impossible; for the odds were certainly against him. By graduating from Hampton, he had begun to break the cycle that produces poverty and illiteracy. Every Charles Everett after him has been a college graduate; thus, moving the family closer to the realization of life, liberty and the pursuit of happiness.

Charles, Jr. participated in extracurricular activities and worked while attending Hampton. A devout Baptist, he participated in the Sunday school program on campus. His school records indicate that his Sunday school teachers were Miss Showers, 1890, Miss Freeman, 1891, and Mr. Turner, 1894-95. He also participated in the Institute Battalion for three years and reached the rank of sergeant.

During the years 1890-92, he worked on the farm there, and from 1893-95 earned his tuition by rendering janitorial service.

When Hampton celebrated its twenty-seventh anniversary, among the members of the graduating class was C. P. Everett, Jr. At 1:30 p.m., the ceremony was held in the gymnasium. On the printed program, Charles was listed as a participant. He read his essay entitled "What Hampton Means." A variety of selected music was performed that afternoon: "Tis Morn" by Gieoel, "To God on High" by Mendelssohn, and "Song of the Sea" by Veazie – the chorus of this song was performed by a group of Native American students attending Hampton. Other songs included Balfe's Excelsior", "My Country 'Tis of Thee", and plantation songs.

Graduating Class of 1895, Charles P. Everett, Jr.,
second row from the top, third from the right.

Graduation did not separate him from "Dear Hampton" to which he would return to attend summer sessions in 1895, 1896, 1897, and 1898. He would also write several letters to former teachers and friends who remained at Hampton.

Following his graduation, he entered the teaching profession and joined the ranks of black pioneers who entered a wilderness where he had to blaze an educational trail. In a letter written on November 5, 1895, he indicated that he was teaching in Odessa, Delaware. In that communication to a Miss Bellows, he described a dearth of instructional materials and requested assistance. He asked her to send instructional items with which he could keep the little ones busy. The children whom he taught seemed to have enjoyed poetry more than any other literary form. Except for this letter, there is no other known information available about his experiences in Odessa.

In the year 1896, he was encouraged to come to Alabama where he would enter a world that was more hostile to black people than where he had been. In 1890, 1894 and 1896, there had been three known incidents where black citizens had been lynched. In Caswell County from where his father had escaped enslavement, one African American lynching is recorded, and that was in 1885. This form of documented terrorism would be a part of the landscape facing black people in all the counties where he would work in Alabama. Among the most salient impediments that he would face in rural Montgomery County, were little or no public funding for educating children, which resulted in inadequate or no facilities in which to establish a school, and a paucity of tools and supplies with which to work. Religious leaders and their congregations would offer their church buildings as spaces where teaching and learning could take place. Desks, books, and other essentials were often not affordable. He would also be greeted by well entrenched "Jim Crow" laws. In 1896, the Supreme Court ruled in Plessey v. Ferguson that segregation was constitutional and established the doctrine that races were equal but must remain separate in education and public accommodations.

In spite of this, he accepted the opportunity to do what good that he could. He would join other pioneer educators with a Hampton connection like Booker T. Washington, the principal of Tuskegee Institute in Macon County, Miss Charlotte Thorn and Miss Mable Dillingham, leaders at the Calhoun School in Lowndes County and Miss Georgia Washington, who had established the People's Village School in Mount Meigs in 1893. It was also in 1896, that Professor Washington brought George Washington Carver to Tuskegee to head the Agricultural Department.

Together they would find ways and means by which they would overcome the many obstacles impeding the development of effective educational programs in the rural Black Belt, an area blessed with black fertile soil which was very suitable for planting a variety of crops. My grandfather found in the small rural village of Mount Meigs, Alabama located approximately twelve miles east of Montgomery, a supportive Black community, and a tolerant White citizenry. It would be Miss Georgia Washington who would serve as a beacon light to guide him for the three years that he worked in her service.

In a report sent to Hampton Agricultural and Industrial Institute in 1897, Miss Washington made extensive reference to Charles P. Everett, Jr.:

> "The term just past has been the most helpful of any previous year. Captain Everett's work for the last two years in the classroom has been the making of our school. Our first class of five members will graduate next term, three of whom are now teaching summer schools, in order to get some practical help in their future work, before finishing up their last term in school here. The school's enrollment for the last term was two hundred and twenty-five with an attendance of two hundred and fifteen. Quite a number of these children came to school for the first time to us, many old scholars were obliged to stay out and work, with the thought of coming back next term. This of course hinders the classroom work a great deal, for it simply means to go over the same ground once again in the teaching. Many of the scholars who came and had not money, brought what they had at home to pay for their schooling, such as chickens, eggs, butter, milk, sweet potatoes, pork, meal and flour. Two of the girls cared for the lady teachers' rooms, one boy for the gentleman's' room. Four boys cared for the schoolhouse,

People's Village School Building (Circa 1896)

Besides the two hundred and twenty-five scholars in the day school, fifteen men of families made up a class in night school taught by Captain Everett. Captain Everett also has a conference of twenty-five men, who meet twice a month to talk up the subject of farming. The men were quite interested in the discussion, such as, why we plow? How we plow? How to make the soil produce more?"[5]

Listed as members of the Board of Trustees on the Sixth Annual Report are the following individuals:

Mr. Frederick Johnson, President – Mt. Meigs, Alabama
Mr. Lewis Pierce, Vice President – Mt. Meigs, Alabama
Mr. J. H. Smothers – Secretary – Mt. Meigs, Alabama
Prof. William Burns Patterson – Montgomery, Alabama
Mr. Hilliard Pinkston – Mt. Meigs, Alabama
Mr. Brake Lucas – Mt. Meigs, Alabama
Mr. Armstead Brown – Pike Road, Alabama

[5] The Fifth Annual Report of the Principal of the People's Village School; Mount Meigs Village, Montgomery Co., Alabama; 1897.

Prof. Booker T. Washington – Tuskegee, Alabama
Dr. J. C. Nicholson – Mt. Meigs, Alabama

As noted in the makeup of the Board of Trustees, Miss Washington believed in surrounding herself with other strong pioneer educators. Professor William Burns Patterson and Professor Booker T. Washington had experience in organizing educational programs. In 1871, Patterson, a white emigrant from Tullibody, Scotland, had organized the Tullibody Academy for Negroes in Greensboro, Alabama, and helped to establish the Lincoln School and Normal University in Marion, Alabama. This program would later be moved to Montgomery, Alabama and become the Alabama State Normal School for Colored Students. She would also draw from the experiences of Professor Booker T. Washington who had developed the Tuskegee Normal and Industrial Institute in 1881.

The report lists the following teachers:

Georgia Washington – Principal
Martha E. Cooke
Charles P. Everett
Mary Lee McCrary

Each teacher was paid $161.09 for services performed in 1897, and they received $46.01 for board and travel. When converted to 2022 dollars, $161.00 is approximately $3,850.00. The school year lasted eight months. The money for salaries and board was raised from tuition collected from students and donations from various sources. During that year, the price of commodities such as cotton, corn and potatoes had dropped, and share cropping families found it difficult to pay money for tuition; therefore, items such as eggs, chickens, milk products, and sweet potatoes were accepted by Miss Washington and her staff when possible. Some students did chores in the teachers' dormitories to pay for their tuition.

The school was divided into four grade levels: primary; intermediate; junior; and grammar. The curriculum included arithmetic, language, physiology and hygiene, geography and history, social and religious life, and sewing and agriculture.

Getting the school day started was one of the most serious administrative challenges. Many homes did not have clocks; therefore, families had to depend on the rising of the sun to tell the approximate time of day. On cloudy days children would get to school late. In November of 1997, a friend of the mission of the People's Village School donated a large bell which could be heard as far away as eight miles. The entire community began to depend on the ringing of that bell to get the workday started.

Photograph of Students and Staff of People's Village School
at the Beginning of a School Day (Circa 1898)

While residing in the Mount Meigs community, Charles continued to be influenced by his religious roots. He joined the Antioch Baptist Church which was located near the People's Village School campus. That church had been organized in 1819 when Alabama had become a state. The original membership was comprised of whites, some of whom enslaved African Americans. On Sunday mornings, he taught Sunday school there, and since the school and the church were so closely connected, he would help lead the Christian Endeavor meeting between four and five o'clock p.m. in the large assembly room of the school building. He would draw from his musical training at Hampton in teaching the children and adults the diverse songs he had learned. The church had also recognized his leadership ability and appointed him to membership on the Board of Deacons.

Antioch Baptist Church (Circa 1896)

Charles P. Everett, Jr. continued to work with Miss Washington until 1899. In a letter written on June 23, 1899, to Dr. Frissell of Hampton Institute, he indicated that he was teaching summer school in the town of Tuskegee, Alabama. By November 27, of that year, he reported in another letter to Dr. Frissell, that he had been called to teach in Panther Creek, Alabama then located twenty miles from Mt. Meigs. This community was in Bullock County. He indicates that he had gained the good will of white men in the community who were willing to sell land for the building of a school that he was planning to call Armstrong Industrial High School. He also stated in that letter that a Reverend Silas Jones was the Pastor in charge of the church building in which he was teaching. Reverend Jones was very supportive of building a graded school. He was not a stranger to building schools.

While serving as pastor of the Saint James Baptist Church in Waugh, Alabama in 1887, he and his Board of Deacons had assisted Miss Cornelia Bowens in establishing the Mt. Meigs Institute in 1888. There were over five hundred children of school age within three miles of the Panther Creek community.

On November 14, 1902, he wrote a letter to a Miss Sherman at Hampton and indicated that he was still teaching and had succeeded in purchasing five acres of land for a school which had been incorporated under the name Armstrong Industrial High School of Reynolds in Bullock County, Alabama. According to Alabama Corporates Company Profiles, the incorporation occurred on September 30, 1902, and is assigned Company Number 708-530.[6] In that letter he stated that there were several apt boys and girls under his tutelage who were interested in attending Hampton. There is no information available about his career in Bullock County.

During this period of his life, he seemed to have been able to stay focused on his mission of providing agricultural education to the families of the rural Black Belt communities. There, African Americans' main form of transportation was by horse and wagon. He seemed not to have been distracted by the social upheavals that were occurring in the nearby urban community of Montgomery where there had been a struggle for equal treatment of blacks and whites on the public transit system. The Lightning Route Electric Trolley System was in its fourteenth year of operation. Montgomery was the birthplace of this mode of transportation on April 15, 1886. From 1900 to 1902, Black passengers had boycotted this system because of the separate and unequal treatment on the trollies. The Supreme Court had promised "equal but separate" accommodations on public modes of transportation the year that Charles P. Everett, Jr. had come to Montgomery County; however, the white leaders in charge of the City of Montgomery did not govern by the ruling of the United States Supreme Court. The black protesters were not successful in their first boycott attempt. There

---

[6] Alabama Corporates Company Profiles: AlabamaCorporates.com, 2013.

would not be another effort put forth until December 5, 1955, when the Montgomery Bus Boycott occurred.

Despite a busy career as a pioneer educator in the Black Belt of Alabama, he met and fell in love with Maggie Lee Gee (Ghee). She was one of the two daughters of Joe and Malinda Thompson Gee (Ghee). On December 30, 1903, he and Maggie were joined in marriage. Reverend John Brannan was the officiant at the wedding. They resided in Mt. Meigs after they were married. On July 9, 1912, Charles P. Everett, Jr. (III) was born, and his father became C. P. Everett, Sr.

On October 15, 1917, Superintendent J. A. Coleman, recommended the employment of Professor Charles P. Everett, Sr. to the Lowndes County, Board of Education. The following Board members were in attendance: J. R. Collins, L. D. James, S. W. Holloday, and J. D. Reese. He was hired to teach vocational education at Lowndes County Training School. That year the Board determined that students would attend school sixty days rather than eighty days beginning on the first day of December rather than the first day of October; this was because of conservation efforts brought on by World War I. At a meeting held on October 4, 1918, the Board hired Maggie Gee Everett to teach home economics at Lowndes County Training School. That same year, Charles P. Everett, Jr. (III) entered first grade.

Charles P. Everett, Jr., left, on the campus of Lowndes Co. Training School with unidentified white gentleman (Circa 1925)

Maggie Gee Everett on the Campus of Lowndes
County Training School (Circa 1925)

Lowndes County Training School was located seven miles southwest of Hayneville, Alabama in the Mosses Community; it was also thirty miles southwest of Montgomery, Alabama. The first school building was constructed in 1913; and its first two principals were Mrs. Mary F. Edwards and Mr. S. T. Wilson. By 1925, additional land was purchased and a vocational department and living quarters for the teachers were added. When Professor Wilson resigned, Charles P. Everett, Sr. (Jr.) was promoted to the position of principal.

The Everett family lived on campus in the teacherage. While residing in the Mosses Community of Hayneville, he continued his pattern of being involved in the church by serving at Mount Moriah Baptist Church # 1. In 1921, during the pastorate of Reverend C. C. Smedley, he served as the superintendent of the Sunday school. As he walked to church from the campus of the school, he would recruit children to join him and his family in Sunday school thus emphasizing the importance of the triad of the family, the church, and the local school.

On November 20, 1928, when R. E. Tidwell was State Superintendent of Education, Charles P. Everett, who was serving as principal teacher and vocational educator, applied for a permanent teaching certificate. In a letter from Mr. P. W. Hodges, Secretary Division of Teacher Training, Certification and Placement, he was given the following instructions:

"Please send the transcript form to the registrar of Hampton Institute with the request that it be filled and signed to indicate your graduation and then secure from Tuskegee Institute on blanks of the kind which have been sent to the registrar statements of credits earned in the institution within the last three years. All these blanks properly executed by you and the registrars of the two institutions must be accompanied to the State Department of Education by a remittance of $2.00 in postal money order, cashier's check, or currency and by statements from your employers to the effect that you have taught satisfactorily the subject of vocational agriculture for at least four years in the schools of Alabama."

On November 24, 1928, Charles sent a letter to Hampton. In that communication he explained that he was attempting to secure a better certificate as a principal and vocational teacher. He declares the following in that letter:

"I am asking you the favor to fill in as much to my credit as you can possibly bear. I believe I spent a splendid period there and feel that my Alma Mater will do all she can to hold up her product.

I am not sure as to who is there now, but Dr. R. R. Moton of Tuskegee knows all about my stay there at Hampton. Major Allen Washington also knows about me." Dr. Moton had taught Charles at Hampton and had become the Principal of Tuskegee Normal and Industrial Institute following Booker T. Washington's death.

On December 4, 1928, the Secretary of Appointments at Hampton sent the following information to Mr. R.E Cammack at the State Department of Education:

"At the request of Charles P. Everett, R.F.D. 2, Box 49, Hayneville, Alabama, I enclose a transcript of the work he had at Hampton Institute.

He made a good record, and we understand has done well in Alabama."

My grandfather continued to serve as principal of Lowndes County Training School until failing health caused him to offer his resignation in 1937. His unexpired term was carried out by Mr. L. R. Grasham.

CHAPTER 3

CHARLES P. EVERETT, JR., SR. (III)

MY FATHER WAS BORN ON JULY 12, 1912, IN MOUNT MEIGS, Alabama., three years after his grandfather had passed away.

Charles P. Everett, Jr. (III) top row first on left (1), and his Friends.
Annie Dove (Thomas) is on the bottom row in the Center (4). They
are on the Campus of Lowndes County Training School
(Vocational Building in the background and School
Building to the left of Charles) (Circa 1921)

Samuel Bradley was one of my father's good friends. Both began their first-grade experience in 1918. In an interview that I had with him on March 1, 2000, he indicated that he had lived in the Stones

Community which was located two- and one-half miles away from Lowndes County Training School, and that he would walk that distance barefoot. When the weather was cold, his parents provided him with rubber boots to keep his feet warm. He stated that he and Charles had entered the first grade the same year, and both graduated from high school in 1929. He remembered Professor Everett's administrative leadership. In the tradition of Hampton Institute and People's Village School, Professor Everett would ring the bell to begin the school day. He stated that the bell would toll three times. The first tolling would occur at seven o'clock a.m., the second at seven thirty a.m. and the third at eight a.m. Students were expected to be on time and dressed in uniform. They would assemble on the campus and march into the school building with their teachers.

Annie Dove Thomas, another close friend also remembered hearing the school-opening bell as she made her five-mile trek from the Beechwood Community. She and her brothers and sisters would cover the distance of ten miles to and from school and arrive on time because they did not want to encounter the wrath of Professor Everett. She declared that on some occasions, she would be able to ride to school on a horse-drawn wagon driven by her uncle.

In 1929, Sam Bradley and my father graduated from Lowndes County Training School. They both matriculated at Tuskegee Institute. A vocational school for Negro youth, it offered four-year college courses in the following areas: Agriculture, Home Economics, Technical Arts, Business and Education leading to the Bachelor of Science degree. It also offered two-year college courses in Business Practice, Teacher-Training, Manual Arts and Home Economics.

According to Mr. Bradley, they lived in Emery Hall Number 4, one of a group of 4 dormitories situated along Moton Drive on the southwest side of the campus. Moton Drive was named for R. R. Moton who was previously mentioned in this narrative. Dormitory life was challenging for those who boarded there. He indicated that bed bugs were a constant menace, and that they infested his residence hall. He would complain to the matron of the dorm, Ms. J. R. Otis but because of the lack of insecticides at that time very little could be done. The

Institute laundry service would see to it that bed linen was washed properly, but the expression, "Sleep tight and don't let the bed bugs bite," was appropriate in this case. Matrons gave instruction in how to prepare the bed properly for sleeping by tightening the sheets to prevent being bitten by insects. Mr. Bradley said he started to leave school because of the problem with bed bugs. In some communities, wealthy people were able to put their mattresses in large ovens periodically to kill bed bugs, but that was not the case at Tuskegee Institute in the 1920s and '30s.

Daddy and Mr. Bradley earned money to help pay fees by performing janitorial service or working on the farm or in the cafeteria at Tompkins Hall. When they were not working, they filled their leisure time by playing cards and quartet singing. Daddy declared Agriculture and Science as a major emphasis of study and English as a minor. In addition to his academic load, he also found time to play football and sing in the Tuskegee Institute Choir.

On December 27, 1932, he sang in the choir under the leadership of William Levi Dawson in the gala opening of Radio City Music Hall. He was fond of telling the story about riding on an elevator with members of the bass section of the Don Cossack Singers. He stated that as they descended from their hotel room to the lobby, the Russians began to warm-up for their performance. The deep resonance of their singing caused the elevator and everything in it to vibrate powerfully.

Charles Everett, III, back row and 6ᵗʰ from the left

Experiencing New York City and participating in the opening of Radio City Music Hall was certainly a high point for my father in 1932. That same year he experienced one of his lowest points. He reported that while sitting on his bed in Emery Hall Number 4, he had a vision. In it, he was attending his mother's funeral and that while riding in the funeral procession a car had broken down and could be observed parked on the side of the road. He was prescience because a few days later he received word that his mother, Maggie Gee Everett had passed away.

Annie Dove Thomas reported to me that Mrs. Everett had become ill with what she described as the eight-day pneumonia. Mrs. Thomas stated that Maggie's sister Dora Jarrett had come from Mount Meigs to help. Professor Everett had summoned Annie and her mother to come to the teacherage on the campus of Lowndes County Training School to assist with Grandmother Maggie. On that cold and rainy night, he would drive from Mosses to Hayneville to get Dr. Mollet, a white physician to provide medical care. Shortly after receiving treatment Maggie Everett died.

Following her funeral, she was buried in a grave in Mount Meigs on the Antioch Plains near Highway 80. Daddy said that during the funeral procession, a car did breakdown as he had seen in the vision at Tuskegee.

On May 25, 1933, Tuskegee held its Forty-eighth Commencement Exercises. On that day, according to an article in The Tuskegee Messenger: "One -hundred thirty-three young men and women marched across the platform of Logan Hall to receive from the hands of Principal R. R. Moton, degrees, diplomas and certificates. An early edition of The Southern Letter records that 'fully five hundred persons came from Montgomery, Tuskegee and all parts of Macon County to attend the Commencement.' This year 3,500 people from all over the South and many from the North filled Logan Hall to capacity while close upon 2,000 more strolled up and down the roads through the campus, sat around upon the grass, crowded the community stores, or chatted around refreshment booths. It was a 'big day' for the Negroes of Macon County – Commencement at the 'Normal School.'"[7]

The center piece of "Big Day" was the Baccalaureate and Commencement Exercises. In both events Charles P. Everett, Jr. (III), like his father, performed in the choir. Under the direction of Mr. Dawson, the choir sang the following anthems: "I Heard of a City Called Heaven" by Johnson, "Behold God the Lord" by Mendelssohn. Other melodies that were sung by choir and audience were: "Let the Heaven Light Shine on Me," "Lead Me, Lead Me, My Lord," and "We Are Climbing Jacob's Ladder." The speaker for the occasion was Dr. M. Ashley Jones, Honorary President of the Commission on Interracial Cooperation in Atlanta, Georgia.

The choir and orchestra were also heavily involved in the Commencement Exercises at 10:30 a.m. and 2:00 p.m. The following selected music was performed at the morning Exercise: "Sun Down," "Been Down Into the Sea," "Good News," and "Soon I Will Be Done."

Featured in the afternoon program in Logan Hall were: "Largo" by Handel, "Tuskegee Song," "Sylvia," and "Great Day."

The Commencement Address was delivered by Dr. John Hope, President of Atlanta University, Atlanta, Georgia.[8]

The Tuskegee Messenger reported that the life of philanthropist, Mr. Julius Rosenwald was celebrated on that occasion. Mr. Rosenwald who had served as a trustee at Tuskegee for twenty years, passed away on January 6, 1932. Known for his support of education for the Negros of the South, he had built ten schools in Macon County. While touring the Black Belt on another occasion, he had visited Miss Georgia Washington on the campus of the People's Village School in Montgomery County.[9]

That year my father would join the growing number of black men and women who were becoming teachers. The Tuskegee Messenger declared in the article titled, "Teachers Increase More Than Fifty Per

---

[7] "Commencement at Tuskegee Institute: "Big Day" in Macon County" The Tuskegee Messenger, Vol. IX No. 6, Tuskegee Institute, May 1933, p. 1.

[8] Ibid., p. 4.

[9] Ibid., p. 8.

Cent in the Last Decade," that in 1920, there were 6,253 male and 29,189 female Negro teachers in the United States. By 1930 that number had risen to 8,767 males and 45,672 females. In Alabama, the trend was similar. There were 442 male and 2,010 female in 1920, but by 1930 the number had grown to 599 male and 3,571 female.[10]

His journey as an educator would begin with certification in agriculture, science, and English. Mr. J. A. Coleman, Superintendent, recommended his hiring to the Lowndes County Board of Education. This they did and during the 1933-34 school year, he joined his father's faculty at his high school alma mater, the Lowndes County Training School. He would serve under his father's leadership for three years. The joy of returning to work there would have been complete if his mother had been there to welcome him physically as a colleague. He could only rely on his memories of her to sustain him. In 1935, he would leave his position as a teacher in Lowndes County.

During the 1936 - 37 school year he was hired by the Pike County Board of Education. He would serve there as a principal teacher until 1941.

By the 1941-42 academic year, Charles and Minnie Everett were employed by the Autauga County Board of Education. Though grateful for the opportunity to be gainfully employed and have the opportunity to work together in the same county, they would be greeted by adversity.

---

[10] Ibid., p. 13.

Momma and Daddy in front of North Highland circa 1944

Working under Jim Crow laws, policies and mores would prove to be a struggle they would have to overcome. The first impediment was the disparity in the length of the school year for black and white schools. According to the Board of Education minutes, in 1940 white schools opened on September 9. The colored high school opened on September 23. The colored elementary schools opened on October 7.[11] By March of 1942 that disparity was still evident. The Board voted that the length of the school year for white elementary schools was 160 days and high schools 164 days. That year the colored secondary schools would be in session for 150 days and elementary schools for 140 days.[12]

Despite these disparities, Charles was able to climb the employment ladder by being appointed principal of North Highland High School in 1944. One of the first problems that he faced was managing the closing of some smaller one-room school buildings and the consolidating of the students and staffs into North Highland which would operate on a first through twelfth grade configuration. To accommodate that model the Board of Education acquired the Lutheran school building located on

---

[11] Minutes of the Autauga County Board of Education for August 5, 1940.
[12] Minutes of the Autauga County Board of Education for March 11, 1942.

Sixth Street. That building with its four classrooms became the North Highland Annex and housed the first and second grades. I attended North Highland Elementary Annex and remember spending two academic-years in that white clapboard structure. The two first-grade rooms were on the front of the structure. The two rear rooms housed the second grade and contained in that space was an adjourning stage for assembly programs which would include plays and musical productions. Mrs. Delilah Goshe was my first-grade teacher. Mrs. Carrie Benson taught me in second grade.

The Lutheran Mission allowed the Board to use that building for instruction without ownership by the Autauga County Board of Education. It was not until 1949 that the school building would be purchased. At a Board meeting held on April 21, 1949, Mr. E. E. Krebs of the Lutheran Church read a letter accepting the bid of the County Board of Education in the amount $5,000.00.

Grades three through twelve were housed in a newly renovated building on Chestnut Street. My father's challenge there was to configure that building to support the core curriculum. On the south side of the structure English, mathematics and social studies classes were taught. Science was taught on the south wing of the building. The self-contained elementary classrooms were located on the north wing. Each room was designed so that it contained a cloakroom space that served multiple purposes which included timeout for unruly students and a storage area.

On the east side was the entrance to the building that led into a central corridor. On each side of the hallway were movable walls that could be closed to create smaller classrooms for elective courses. Periodically, this area would be opened to accommodate a space for assembly activities and after-school social events.

On a hill on the north side of the campus, an older unpainted clapboard structure was converted into a lunchroom, and classrooms were added to that facility to accommodate home economics and agricultural instruction.

Funding for the purchase of supplies and equipment to support the instructional program was the most salient challenge. Daddy told me that when he was hired to be principal, the superintendent met him at the Autauga County Courthouse where the central office was located. Following a school opening conference, the superintendent gave him a box of chalk and some erasers and said: "Have a good year Professor." All other instructional supplies and equipment had to be obtained through fund raising activities. Those activities included various PTA projects, the showing of movies, operating a school sweet shop and sponsoring school dances. Claude Shannon and his band named the House Rockers and Bobby Jackson were favorites for performing at the dances.

In 1956, Daddy resigned as principal of North Highland and returned to Lowndes County where he taught science at the Lowndes County Training School when R. R. Pearce was principal there. He would later be hired as principal of Prentice High in Montevallo, Alabama; this community was in the Shelby County School System. Circa 1966, he returned to the Autauga County School System.

In 1976, my father retired there as a Guidance Counselor, basketball coach and bus driver at Marbury High School. That year, he was interviewed by Keith Jackson, a writer for The Montgomery Monitor. In the article titled "Teaching Has Been Wonderful to Us", Daddy summarized the apotheosis of his career in education thusly: "One of the greatest joys I got was the chance to work on the faculty during my last years with three of my former students."[13]

---

[13] Jackson, Keith (1976, June 23) Teaching Has Been Wonderful for Us. *The Montgomery Monitor*, p. 6.

CHAPTER 4

MINNIE SMITH EVERETT

IN MY FAMILY'S JOURNEY, THE MATRIARCHS HAVE MADE SIGNIFICANT strides toward life, liberty and the pursuit of happiness. In 1866, after Charles P. Everett, Sr. had won the right to vote under the Fourteenth Amendment to the U. S. Constitution, Mary, his wife, and other Black women had not achieved suffrage. That would not translate into reality until the Nineteenth Amendment was ratified on August 18, 1920. My mother, Minnie Louise Smith was born on November 4, 1914, before suffrage was attained. She was the daughter of Hugh Smith and Sallie Miles Smith in Hayneville, Alabama. She was the granddaughter of Levi Miles (1845-1913) and Sallie Rudolph Miles (1860-1930).

She was reared in the home of her maternal grandmother, the widow, Sallie Rudolph Miles. Levi Miles, Sr. died on August 13, 1913, and Sallie Rudolph Miles was left to rear many of the grandchildren and other relatives. She had been born into slavery in the Hayneville area. Described as a tall and slender woman with brown complexion, she possessed a voice that projected well. Momma indicated that she was a firm disciplinarian as validated in her following story about being brought up under Sallie's guidance: It appears that John T. Miles one of the sons of John Miles had stolen an item from the store of a local merchant in Hayneville, who had reported the matter to Sallie Rudolph Miles. Sallie summoned all the children and grandchildren into the front bedroom of her home which was located near Court Square in that small Alabama county seat. After having required the gathering to sit on the floor around that room, she grabbed John T. who was about ten years old and tied a rope around one of his legs; the other end of the rope was thrown across one of the exposed beams in the ceiling area of the room. After having drawn John T. into the air up-side-down, she took the loose end of the rope and tied it around the post of an old-oak bed. With a stick in-hand she began to beat him. He screamed so loudly that the Sheriff, whose office was located nearby, came running to see what the ruckus was about.

When the Sheriff arrived, he knocked on the front door and was given entry. He admonished the Widow Miles and told her that she would have to stop her actions. She looked at the Sherriff sternly and said, "Sherriff, do you see that oak tree over there", pointing toward the window? 'Well, I want you to go over there and bend it." He responded, "Sallie, you know I can't bend that oak tree.' She replied, "When it was a sapling, you could have bent it, but now that it is grown, you can't do anything with it. Sheriff, I'm bending a sapling." Without returning a mumbling word, the Sheriff departed to his office. Although some may have called her discipline abusive, John T. Miles became a law-abiding citizen and one of the strong and successful men of the Miles family retiring as a steel worker in Birmingham, Alabama.

By 1920, Momma had begun attending Russell Industrial School. It was there that her climb toward parity with the Everett patriarchs would have its genesis. After having completed her first four years of education at Russell, she attended Loveless Junior High School in Montgomery, Alabama where Professor T. A. Randal was her principal. There, she completed her elementary and junior high experience. While in Montgomery, she resided in the home of her maternal Aunt Redry Miles on Sutter Street. One of her neighbors was Miss Willie Marjorie Stone who mentored her at Mount Zion A. M. E. Zion Church on South Holt Street in the Peacock community. Miss Stone was the assistant superintendent of the Sunday school there.

Momma returned to Lowndes County where she attended Lowndes County Training School where Professor Charles P. Everett, Jr. was her principal. She maintained a high academic standard in grades nine through 12 by earning credit in the following subjects: English, algebra, plane geometry, physics, history, civics, biology, chemistry, and home economics. She was also a member of the school chorus, the girls' basketball team, and drama and 4H clubs. After graduation she earned a license to work as a hairdresser. She matriculated at Alabama State Teachers College from 1938-41 and qualified for a provisional teaching certificate.

As stated earlier in this narrative, she began teaching in Prattville, Alabama at North Highland. She taught fifth grade there. From conversations I have had with her students, she was described by them as kind, understanding and loving. In her classroom, the students saw her as a mother figure who was there for them in times of sadness with comforting words. She encouraged those who had become discouraged. She seemed to have found joy in doing things for others whether small or large. Her students' reflections focused on how she helped the underprivileged children by supplying them with food, and clothing.

In 1944, she witnessed an important action taken by the Autauga County Board of Education in support of teaching and learning when the first Jeanes Teacher was appointed. The purpose of this position was to provide instructional leadership. The Jeanes Foundation provided resources that helped teachers to be more effective when working in African American rural communities. Teachers in the program were called supervising industrial teachers, Jeanes supervisors, Jeanes agents, or Jeanes teachers. These teachers had broad latitude to decide what areas to focus on in their individual communities. It was also understood that community needs were different, and teachers' methods would vary. Jeanes teachers also worked to raise money for schools, purchase school equipment and to advocate for extending instructional time. Supervising teachers were chosen by county superintendents.[14] On October 26, 1944, the Superintendent recommended the hiring of Rose Lewis Lott as Jeanes teacher with a salary being fixed at $110.00

---

[14] Jeanes Foundation (June 13, *2020*, at 5:34 (UTC). In *Wikipedia*. Retrieved from URL.

per month and travel allowance of $40.00 per month for nine months.[15] She was based at North Highland on the Chestnut Street campus.

Left to right Mary Bracy, Rose Lewis Lot (Jeanes Teacher),
Minnie Everett standing in front of North Highland circa 1944

In 1950, Momma earned a BS Degree in Elementary Education from Alabama State Teachers College and a Master of Education there in 1956.

During this period, she witnessed the landmark decision Brown v. Board of Education which overruled Plessy v. Ferguson in 1954. With this important action, members of the Everett Family saw a glimmer of hope. It marked another step toward life, liberty, and the pursuit of happiness. This Supreme Court Case determined that racial segregation in public schools was unconstitutional.

While working under segregated restrictions, Momma was able to identify discriminatory instructional practices in the classrooms of Autauga County, Alabama. In her master's theses, <u>Negro Life and History in Social Studies Courses in the Elementary Schools of Autauga County, Alabama 1955 – 1956</u>, she made these disparities known. The following were salient among her findings:

1. "All literature implied a need for the inclusion of unbiased facts about Negro achievement in textbooks, newspapers, and other

---

[15] Minutes of the Autauga County Board of Education for October 26, 1944.

periodicals, these authors also revealed very limited coverage of Negro life in textbooks. That which was included was biased and presented the Negro according to a characteristic pattern. He was represented as being suited for hot climates, happy-go-lucky, illiterate, and unable to care for himself.

2. Teachers represented in the study have adequate training. Eighteen or 82 per cent hold college degrees. Two or 9 per cent have Master of Education degrees and two or 9 percent have attained three years of college training.

3. Other data on teachers are not as favorable. They had taken only three courses on Negro life in professional school. Twelve or 55 per cent had had Negro history; eight or 36 per cent had taken Negro literature. Four or 18 per cent had taken a course in education with special emphasis on the Negro.

4. The most popular topics covered were sport, music, entertainment, and science. The least popular were art, armed forces, business, industry, and labor.

5. Teachers have few books in the libraries. Ten or 45 per cent have Negro Caravan, seven have Up from Slavery and four or 19 percent have Life of Carver.

6. A qualitive evaluation of included material revealed that factual material on Negroes was inadequate in terms of attitudes conveyed. The material is biased in treatment, it presents characteristic stereotypes, and no factual material is included on the contributions of Negroes in the total cultural development of American civilization.

7. A qualitative analysis of textbooks revealed insufficient Negro coverage in factual material and illustrations by lines." [16]

---

[16] Everett, Minnie S. (1956, August) Negro Life and History in the Social Studies Courses in the Elementary Schools of Autauga County, Alabama 1955 – 1956. Unpublished, pp. 102, 103 and 105.

She offered the following recommendations to solve the identified problems:

1. "Participating teachers should use the evidence presented in this study as a challenge to enrich their curriculum with Negro life. Currently, the teaching of Negro achievements rest almost wholly with the teachers themselves. It is, therefore suggested that all teachers would obligate themselves to learn more facts about Negro contributions themselves, as well as present more to their students.

2. The curriculum of Negro life be broad in the scope of factual coverage. It should include a variety of teaching techniques and materials.

3. Such methods should include experience units, projects on Negro life. These should be correlated with other subjects, socialized recitation, research, and audio-visual methods.

4. Textbooks should present the Negro in an unbiased manner and not in the characteristic role of a menial servant, happy-go-lucky, lazy person.

5. There should be adequate coverage of Negro life in textbooks, both qualitatively and quantitatively."[17]

She not only applied this research to her instructional practices in her classroom at North Highland, but in her home. At 18 (later 746) Glass Street, Ronnie, I, and other children found a print-rich environment relative to Negro literature in the form of magazines, storybooks, and other materials. Negro History Week found her involved at home, in the Mount Zion A.M.E. Zion Church and the Community House on Union Street where her Federated club sponsored programs for children of the community.

Momma continued to be a classroom teacher at North Highland Elementary School until 1959 when she was promoted to principal there. The following individuals served on her instructional staff that year:

---

[17] Everett, pp. 102 – 107.

Jean Lowe Alexander, Alma Williams Bradford, Mary Jean Cillie, Mary Alice Howard, Lizzie Hoyt, Julia Mae Phelps, and Willola Wagstaff. Under her leadership, the instructional staff was desegregated in 1967 when Elenore Webb, a White instructor joined the faculty. Thus, she became the first principal in our family to supervise a desegregated school staff. When Autauga County became a unitary school system North Highland Elementary was closed. She was assigned to be the assistant principal at Prattville Elementary for a short period of time. Her last leadership assignment of her fifteen years as a supervising principal was at Autaugaville Elementary School in Autaugaville, Alabama. In 1976, she retired from the Autauga County School System.

CHAPTER 5

CHARLES P. EVERETT, JR., (IV)

In 1947, Minnie S. Everett, requested and was granted a maternity leave by the Autauga County Board of Education to give birth to her first baby. On April 10th of that year, I was born. The time of arrival was 7:30 p.m. at the Fraternal Hospital on Dorsey Street. Dr. R.E. Tisdale, M.D. performed the delivery, and he was assisted by Mrs. M. M. Lee, R.N.

Mamma was meticulous in keeping a record of events surrounding my birth in a booklet titled <u>Baby's Own Story Year by Year.</u> In that booklet, she recorded many details, and these included individuals who gave me gifts. Listed among them was Mr. E. D. Nixon who gave me a one-dollar bill. Mr. Nixon was a longtime friend of the family. He was instrumental in helping Daddy find summer employment as a sleeping car porter.

It was ironic that I was born on Dorsey Street which was located on the old Peacock Tract section of Montgomery, Alabama. This area was named for the Michael Peacock who enslaved Black people on his antebellum plantation. Had I been born one hundred years earlier, I may have been one of the human beings enslaved there; however, I would grow up in a Montgomery, Alabama that was about to transform the nation in civil rights. The winds of change nationally were already blowing. Just five days after my birth, Jackie Robinson, age 28, became the first African American to play Major League Baseball as a first baseman for the Brooklyn Dodgers.

When my parents brought me home from the hospital, I would reside with them, and my maternal grandmother, Sallie Miles, at our home on 18 (later 746) Glass Street

Charles, Jr., Sr., III and Charles, Jr. (IV) at 746 Glass Street in 1947

This community was a perfect place for me to grow up because it was self-contained. Everything of importance was within walking distance from where we lived. Our place of worship, Mount Zion A. M. E. Zion Church, was located three blocks away at 657 South Holt Street. My parents had joined Mount Zion in 1942 when Reverend C. W. Turn was Pastor. Between the house and the church, the following businesses were located: Neal Conger's Grocery Store, above the store was Dr. Smiley's Dental Office. Across the street on one corner were John Oliver's Gas Station and Garage, Arrington's Barber and Beauty

Shop which stood next door to Arrington's Sweet Shop, and L. D.'s Shoe Repair Shop.

On the southeast corner was Pitt's Drug Store and Soda Fountain. From there, and headed north on Holt Street was the Icehouse, The First C. M. E Church, a Dairy Delight Ice Cream Shop, a U. S. Post Office, Hooper's Shoe Repair Store, Cherry's Apothecary, Lees' Funeral Home, A. L. Long's News Stand, Howard and Howard Funeral Home, the Carver Movie Theater, two more grocery stores, a record shop and two juke joints. I received my first haircut at age one at the Arrington Barber and Beauty Shop.

Other businesses where we enjoyed trading were located a block away on West Jeff Davis Avenue. As I recall, they were Shaw's Bakery, Whites Gas Station, Buster's Barber Shop and Café, Dismuke's Grocery Store, Carter's Cleaners, Dozier's' Appliance Company, Fred Grant's Barber Shop, Scoot's Taxi Stand and Clarence Adams Filling Station. Located in that area were two schools: Loveless School and Jimmy Lowe's Adult School. Fraternal Hospital, already mentioned, Saint Jude Catholic and Addie Payne and Montgomery County Health Department were the medical facilities that served the Peacock community. Many members of the community found employment at the Shirt Factory which was located on Grady Street. As I recall, the only business not available was a bank.

Fraternal Hospital on Dorsey Street, my Place of Birth

Aerial View of the Peacock Tract Circa 1965

While it was convenient to be in proximity to businesses and other important places, life on an unpaved street that did not have sidewalks was challenging. During the dry months of summer, dust became a problem when various motorized vehicles would drive past our home. Dust clouds would permeate the air making breathing difficult. The dust would settle on everything including the houses and vegetation. One of my chores was to take the hose and sprinkle water on the street in front of our home in the morning and again in the evening. The moistened soil emitted a pleasant aroma. Periodically, a municipal truck would spray oil in the street to prevent dust clouds; however, the odor that was produced by that substance was horrible. Rinsing the outer walls of the house was also a chore that my brother Ronnie and I would perform.

Horse-drawn vehicles were common in my neighborhood. Ice and vegetables were delivered by businesses who had not transitioned to motorized forms of transportation. The horses that pulled wagons would defecate in the streets which resulted in foul orders and swarms of flies. From time-to-time the sanitary department of the city would remove the piles of dung, but when the deposit was in front of our home on Glass Street, we would scoop the manure with shovels and deposit it in a field my parents owned. My parents purchased and planted Mimosa trees that released a fragrant aroma in the spring and summer months to mask unpleasant orders. Planting aromatic flowers also helped.

In the late 1950s, the city began updating drainage and sewer systems, and paving streets in the Peacock Tract area. This greatly improved sanitary conditions. By then, horse-drawn vehicles were also fading from use by Montgomery's businesses.

**746 Glass St is 4ᵗʰ house from the right. The dirt
street is being paved circa 1958.**

Chinaberry trees were ubiquitous in our neighborhood. They provided a canopy of abundant shade for our house. Not only did I enjoy climbing those trees, but I was also able to fashion their limbs into imaginary horses. I would use the green berries from the trees for missiles for my slingshots. In the fall and winter months, those berries would become amber in color and fall to the ground. Overtime, they would become fermented. When birds would eat them, they would become disoriented and fly into tree trunks, and the walls of buildings, which was most entertaining for me and my friends to watch.

During the summer months, pests like black and white gnats and mosquitoes became quite a challenge to endure. I thank God that we were able to have aluminum screens installed in our windows and doors to keep them out of our house. In the 1950s air conditioning was non-existent on Glass Street. My father had a creative way of staying cool. He would stop the ice wagon as it was drawn past our home. He would then buy a block of ice from the iceman who would take a pair of tongs and bring the ice to our front porch. Daddy would invert our galvanized washtub and place the block of ice on the base. Behind the tub, he would place an oscillating fan that would blow cool air toward those seated near his creation. My parents did not buy our first window air conditioning unit until the early 1960s.

My 2nd Birthday Party in 1949 (front yard of 18 Glass St.)
I am on the first row and first from right. In the background
is the intersection of Glass and Chilton Streets.

I always felt safe within the Peacock Tract community. There, I was sheltered from the slings and arrows of Jim Crow because I had neighbors who knew me and my family and who were partners with my parents in rearing me. The adults on Glass, Chilton and Holt Streets would chastise me when I needed it and knew that my parents would approve of their efforts.

This feeling of security would be challenged when we would frequently leave our community and walk or drive to other areas of town with my parents. When they were out of town working, my grandmother, whom we called Annie, the daughter of Sallie Rudolph Miles, and I would walk or ride the City Line Bus service downtown for items that could be purchased less expensively than in our neighborhood. On the bus, we were required to sit in the colored only section. However, because we rode on a predominantly Negro route, we had a little more liberty on those buses until we would ride through the white neighborhoods or downtown. Once we debarked the bus on Dexter Avenue, Annie had taught me not to make direct contact with White people. We were also reminded of "our Place" in Jim Crow Montgomery, Alabama, by the ubiquitous "White Only" and "Colored Only" signs over the water fountains, restaurant counters and restroom doors in H.L. Green, Kress, and other department stores.

In April of 1964, I passed the driver's test and received my driver's license. That year my Cousins Bobby and Zack Thomas came from Detroit to visit us. That was their first time in the deep South. I was proud to take them on a site –seeing excursion of the Capitol City of Alabama, and to show off my driving skills. I took them downtown to Dexter Avenue where they were able to see the church edifice that was pastored by the Rev. Dr. Martin Luther King, Jr. It stood in the shadows Goat Hill where the Capitol towered over the surrounding government buildings including the First White House of the Confederacy. I drove them through the Alabama State College campus. From there we traveled to the Upper Wetumpka Road in route toward the State Coliseum and fair grounds. While stopped at a traffic light, a motorcycle cop pulled up next to my car. After breaking, he planted his left foot close to my front-passenger-side tire. In anticipation of the light's changing, I moved forward slightly. He responded in a loud southern drawl, "Nigger, if you hit my foot, I'll blow your damn brains out." Embarrassed and frightened, I waited until he had moved on before I turned and headed back to the safety of the Peacock community.

The only other time that Ronnie and I would leave our community was to take family vacations. Those trips could be contrasted based on the direction. Going north meant that we would be headed away from "Jim Crow." It meant that we would be going to visit with Eugene Smith my maternal uncle who lived in Cleveland, Ohio. Uncle Eugene represented a black person who had left the south and become successful. He was a U. S. Postal mail carrier. He was Republican and had run for congress in the 1960s. Uncle Eugene was well invested in the stock market and would talk for hours about the benefits of putting money in the right places.

Uncle Eugene and his family lived in an upscale-integrated neighborhood with tree-lined streets and well-manicured lawns. His home was a white two-story clapboard structure with a front porch. In the back yard was a lush vegetable garden. He proudly showed us his tomato, okra, and other assorted plants.

Some of the highlights of that trip included attending my first professional-baseball game where the Cleveland Indians played the Kansas City Athletics. It was amazing how chilly a summer night became in that ballpark; It was equally amazing to see and feel how warmly the races interacted with one another in public. He and his children also took us for a wonderful tour of the amusement park at Euclid Beach. It was a much larger scale of the South Alabama Fair which we enjoyed attending back in Montgomery, Alabama at the Garrett Coliseum. It was also free of the racial stress that we left back home.

Ronnie was so fascinated with that spectacular setting that he reached up and grabbed the hand of a white passerby who held his hand and continued to walk several feet with him. Ronnie was completely oblivious to what he was doing until he looked up and realized that he was holding the hand of a stranger and began to cry. We all got a good laugh from that experience.

After staying with Uncle Eugene and his family a few days, we journeyed further north to visit with our cousin Robert Thomas, Jr., the father of the Bobby and Zack who were mentioned earlier. He lived in Detroit, Michigan. Robert, Jr. as he was called had been reared by Annie (my maternal grandmother's nickname) in her home in Hayneville, Alabama. We always thought of him as Mamma's little brother rather than a cousin. Robert was a free-spirited individual who loved to have a good time. While we were in Detroit, he gave up the sporting life to take us on our first visit outside the United States of America. We crossed the northern border and entered Windsor, Ontario, Canada. Ironically, though one thinks of Canada being northward, Windsor is the southernmost city in Canada, and somewhat southeast of Detroit. Culturally, however, it was as far from the "Jim Crow" South as we could get. It was there that I saw a Black man walking together with a Caucasian woman. This was something for which the Negro would have been lynched in some parts of Alabama at the time. We spent the night in our first integrated hotel while touring Windsor. We were truly a long way from home, and I felt safe.

The next day, we drove Robert Jr. back to his home, and began our three-day trip back to Montgomery. In Cincinnati, Ohio, we stopped at the commodious Union Terminal, a great American train station. There we freshened ourselves in preparation for sleeping in the car along the roadside as we made our way back through the segregated South. There would be no hotels available to us as we traveled.

Our church, Mount Zion A.M.E. Zion Church, organized in 1866, was also located within walking distance of our home. I was baptized there on the fourth Sunday of July 1947 by Reverend W. H. Alexander who served as pastor from 1946 to 1948. Mount Zion played a pivotal role in my life, for not only was I Baptized there, but I also met my girlfriend there and would later marry her in that old building that had been erected in 1899. I learned many of my leadership skills while growing up under the guidance of pastors like S. S. Seay, L. Roy

Bennett, S. W. Shultz and Percy Smith, Jr. Miss Willie Marjorie Stone who served as superintendent of the Sunday school was also a mentor. She would often remind me to be my-own-best self.

My family members were my first teachers. Outside of the home, I attended kindergarten at Holt Street Baptist Church where Reverend A. W. Wilson was pastor. Annie would walk with me to Holt Street every day that daycare was in session. I enjoyed attending kindergarten, but I did not like nap- time. Miss Jett, my teacher, would not force me to sleep, and she would read to me while others slept.

In 1951, I began attending elementary school in Prattville, Alabama. Every Sunday night we would leave Annie and Ronnie at our home on Glass Street to drive twelve miles to the faculty apartments on Ninth Street in Prattville Both of my parents told me that when teachers accepted their jobs in Autauga County, they agreed to certain mores. One of those unwritten rules was that educators from Montgomery and other out-side-Autauga County communities were expected to spend the night Monday through Friday in the communities where they taught. This meant paying room and board when staying in the homes of residents or paying rent to live in the apartments built for the faculty of North Highland. That meant that they were also expected to spend their money at businesses in the community.

Teaching and living in that rural community meant giving up some of the comforts of an urban setting. At our home on Glass Street in Montgomery, the source of heating was natural gas. Hot water for bathing, washing clothes, and eating utensils, was readily accessible. The dormitories for teachers, in Prattville, were heated by small potbellied stoves which were fueled by wood and coal. Our home in Montgomery had indoor plumbing which meant that a source of drinking water was always available. Indoor toilet facilities were easily accessible. In Prattville, water had to be hauled into our apartment after having been run into buckets from a spigot on the outside. The water had to be heated on the potbellied stove before being used for bathing. There were no indoor restrooms. All the teachers who resided there had to use a common privy house located in the back yard of the faculty residency.

This activity was especially difficult to perform during the frigid winter months.

Many of the students who attended North Highland came from homes that were more Spartan than the conditions experienced by their teachers. Many of their abodes did not have electricity as a source of power for lighting. They used kerosene fueled lamps at night for reading. Ice boxes were used in place of refrigerators to preserve food. In some cases that resource was not available. Some of those children had to walk long distances to get to school.

In the third grade, I was transferred from the Annex located near Downtown to the main campus on Chestnut Street where Mrs. Julia Mae Phelps was my teacher. Each weekday morning, Daddy would drive in his car from the faculty apartments and park in the south end of the grounds. Standing on the sidewalk at the end of the hedgerow were children waiting to greet my parents and other teachers. They would assist Momma with her packages which would be used in her fifth-grade classroom. The aroma of her perfume, Persian Wool by Avon and her accompanying smile greeted those children every day. Daddy also had something for them to do. He would remove the keys that he carried on his belt and select a student to open the front door of the school building. As I reflect on that daily routine, I believe that my parents were conveying an important message to those scholars: "You are needed, and we trust you."

Because Momma was a teacher on Daddy's faculty, she had gotten into the habit of addressing him as Mr. Everett. Even at home, she referred to him as Mr. Everett. On one occasion, I asked her why she referred to him in such a formal manner. She told me that it was out of respect for his position as principal of North Highland.

The caring attitude of those educators served as a buffer against being educated under difficult physical conditions in the school buildings. North Highland of the 1940s and 1950s did not have many of the conveniences and comforts of our modern comprehensive facilities. The school building was heated by potbellied stoves that were fueled by coal. Unlike the white high schools at Marbury and Prattville, there were no restrooms inside the building. Teachers and students had to trapes out to the back of the campus to use the collection of privy houses that were sectioned off for males and females. The outside water pumps had to be primed to deliver drinking water.

Fieldtrips to Montgomery served a twofold purpose. They were used as fundraising activities, and they provided exposure to the abundance of educational resources available within a short distance from Prattville. Elementary grades three through six would participate in the adventure. It was exciting boarding one of the Greyhound buses that formed the caravan. The itinerary for the 1954 tour included a visit to the Capitol, and the Department of Archives and History.

On one occasion, I had gotten lost in the museum's historical interpretation as projected in the various displays such as the tapestry of the Vine and Olive Settlement, war uniforms and weapons, and bronze statues. I was fascinated by it all; and time had passed by quickly. When I returned to the reality of my situation, I did not hear the voices and footfalls of our tour groups. Looking into the corridor, I didn't see anyone I knew. I ran back into the room where I had been. Dashing to the second-floor window, I gazed out to where the busses were parked and was startled by what I saw. The busses were pulling off in route to the Alaga Syrup Factory. For the first time in my life, I experienced an empty feeling, and I was gripped by fear.

I bounded out of that room, ran down the marble steps, into the spacious foyer and out the huge bronze front door. By then the buses pulled out of their parking spaces and were headed toward Madison Ave. I had a general idea where they were going because I could remember passing the Plant while traveling through North Montgomery in route to our cousin's home. As I ran down Dexter Avenue with tears in my eyes, I was comforted by my familiarity with the stores where my grandmother and I had shopped. When I reached H. L. Green at the corner of Perry and Dexter, I was more aware of my location. When passing Kress Department Store, I was tempted to stop and buy some chocolate covered peanut clusters that Annie had often purchased for me. That thought was only fleeting.

During this whole period, I was ever mindful not to bump into the white shoppers on the crowed sidewalk as I approached the corner of Dexter and Court. There I headed north on Court where I passed Montgomery Fair where my mother often shopped, and where I would sit on Santa's knee at Christmas time. I flashed past Newberry's Five and Dime Store. By that time, I had reached the Corner of Court and Monroe. There I experienced the aromas of food frying at various cafes. Across the street was a huge replica of a shotgun hanging in front of Teague's Hardware.

I continued to run north, until I had reached the enormous Alaga Syrup plant. I didn't see the students or teachers; however, I saw the Greyhound buses lined up in front of the buildings. The drivers were gathered in front of the lead bus where they were laughing and smoking. They didn't notice me. Not knowing how to reunite with my class, teacher, or my mother, I boarded the bus on which I had traveled, found my seat where my sack lunch had not been disturbed. Pausing to catch my breath after the long journey from the Capitol complex, I pondered what form of punishment I would receive for my disobedience in wondering off from my class. Tired, drenched with sweat and worried, I drifted off to sleep. I remember being awakened by the gentle nudge of my teacher.

When I was fully awake and focused, she asked me why I had come to the bus alone. I did not offer an explanation but continued not to make I contact with her. She thought that I had been with Momma and her fifth-grade class. Momma was clueless about what had happened to me. Humbly, I offered an apology for boarding the bus alone. I never told my mother or father about my odyssey on that field trip.

I remained a student in the segregated schools of Autauga County until the end of my third year at North Highland.

In 1955, my parents enrolled me at Saint Jude, Educational Institute in Montgomery. My fourth-grade teacher was Sister Mary Fulgent. The Saint Jude campus was different from that of North Highland in several ways. There were many buildings there including a hospital, church, rectory, nunnery, and school facility. The school building at North Highland was heated by coal in potbellied stoves and the toilets were privies located outside. At Saint Jude the buildings were heated by steam radiators and all of the toilets were inside. Students were required to wear uniforms. The school day often began with mass in the church edifice which was built like a cathedral.

That year was truly a transformative year for me. Since my days at Holt Street Baptist Church Kindergarten, my teachers had been Black. At Saint Jude, most of my instructors were Caucasian. When all around me had been racially segregated, Saint Jude was my transition into a new concept of race relations that would lay the foundation to my future. I was free to look into the eyes of my White teachers. Sister Fulgent did not mind standing close to me and my classmates. During my penmanship class, she would stand next to me, reach across my right shoulder and guide my hand as I labored to form words cursively. She would always smell clean like freshly washed linen.

The distance from my home to Saint Jude was almost two miles. My preferred mode of transportation was to ride the Washington Park bus to Early Street and walk two blocks down Westcott Street and enter the back of the campus and proceed to the church building where I and my friends would gather each morning to begin our school day. Periodically, during good weather, I would walk to school being careful to avoid places where bullies and bad dogs would chase me; there were no leash laws to prevent canines from roaming freely.

1955 was a year that helped to transform my community, the nation, and the world. On December 1st of that year Mrs. Rosa Parks refused to give up her seat to a White passenger on the Cleveland Avenue Bus for which she was arrested. Word of her arrest spread through our community like a wildfire. On Friday night, December 2nd, our pastor, Reverend L. Roy Bennett, who was also president of the Interdenominational Ministerial Alliance, served as chairman of a community meeting that was held at Dexter Avenue Baptist Church. Those attending that meeting gave support to a bus boycott that had been recommended by Ms. Jo Ann Robinson, Mr. E. D. Nixon, and Attorney Fred Gray. By the time of the meeting, Ms. Robinson, an English teacher at Alabama State Teachers College and her students had duplicated copies of a communication encouraging the boycotting of Montgomery City Line buses.

On Sunday morning, all the pews at Mount Zion A.M. E. Zion Church were filled. As I sat there with my family, I listened to Reverend Bennett summarize the events of the week which were centered around the arrest of Rosa Parks that led him to encourage the members to boycott the busses on Monday, December 5, 1955. Those attending gave their enthusiastic support of his request.

That night Momma and Daddy drove back to Prattville leaving Annie, me, and my younger brother Ronnie at our home on Glass Street. As Annie tucked us in, she reminded me that I would need to get a good night's sleep in anticipation of what would occur the next day.

On Monday morning Ronnie and I were awakened to the smell of coffee brewing and Annie's knock at our bedroom door. We bounded out of bed, took our wash up, brushed our teeth and dashed to the kitchen where a scrumptious breakfast had been prepared. Before we could eat, we had to go through our daily ritual lead by Annie: "Alright boys bow your heads and let us pray." After prayer, she would ask us if we had taken our please and thank you pills? We would respond, "No Mam." She would then point to a saucer on the table which contained our invisible please and thank you pills. We would reach toward the saucer and pretend to take our pills after which we would say, "Thank you."

After breakfast, Annie reminded me to get dressed quickly and walk directly to school. She stressed that I was not to ride the bus. As I left the house and began my trek, the weather was cooperative. The temperature was about sixty-four degrees, and there was no rain.

I walked the most direct route which was West Jeff Davis to Oak Street. I noticed that the bus that passed me was empty of passengers. The many other walkers whom I met along the way seemed as enthusiastic as I was. When I got to the church building, my friends ran up to me breathlessly, and asked me how I had gotten to school that morning? I told them that I had walked; to which they responded that it was a good thing that I had done so. When I asked them why they were so alarmed? They told me that if I had ridden the bus that I would have been beaten up by the Boy Scouts. That response had left me in a quandary. Why Boy Scouts would beat bus riders was quite puzzling to me.

After we had assembled in Sister Fulgent's classroom for our morning studies, some of us were still talking about the Boy Scouts. Sister overheard our conversation, chuckled to herself, walked over to the chalkboard, and wrote the word "boycott" in large letters. She said, "This word is pronounced boycott not Boy Scout. It has nothing to do with Boy Scout. That was a relief for me to know. She asked if anyone knew the meaning of the word. One of the girls raised her hand and answered: "It means to stop supporting a business." Sister told her that her answer was correct.

I told the class that I had refused to ride the bus that morning, which caused another student to ask why? Sister went on to explain why the Montgomery City Bus Line was being boycotted. She told the class about Mrs. Rosa Parks who worked as a seamstress at Montgomery Fair Department Store. Since it was the beginning of the Christmas shopping season, Mrs. Parks had worked extremely hard that day sawing clothing for Christmas gifts. When she boarded her bus at the Court Square terminal, she was very tired. Sister declared that according to a description by one of the bus riders: "Mrs. Parks had found a seat in the middle of the bus, where Negroes are allowed to sit, but when the bus became full, and more whites got on the bus with all the seats in the 'white only' section taken, the bus driver told the Negroes who were sitting in the middle section of the bus to get up and move to the back of the bus. On this day there were no seats available in the back. So, the Negroes would have to stand. The bus driver ordered the Negroes to move, but no one moved. Then he told them a second time, and everyone stood except Mrs. Parks."[18]

Sister Fulgent had helped us to understand how unfair the law was for Negro bus riders. This was my first lesson in justifiable civil disobedience and my first look into the face of "Jim Crow." I continued to support the boycott of busses for 382 days. When the weather became too inclement for me to walk, Annie would call Mr. Scott who owned a taxi business in my community, and he would drive me to Saint Jude

---

[18] Yolanda L. Everett, Peter and the Boycott, p. 14, (Bloomington, In.: AuthorHouse Publishing Co., 2014).

School. I experienced the worst weather in January and February of 1956 when the average early morning temperatures were in the upper thirties. The leather outsoles of brown shoes that I wore had become thin and separated from the midsole at the toe tip. I was fortunate that one of our neighbors owned the Hooper Shoe Shop on Holt Street and was available to repair our shoes by replacing the leather outsoles. When I wore the brown shoes or my tennis shoes, my toes would become extremely cold and ache. Adding extra layers of socks would help but cause the shoes to become uncomfortably tight for walking.

While residing in the Peacock Tract community, I was surrounded by heroes and heroines of the protest and would often walk past many landmarks that today are graced by historic markers. The church buildings were the sites where Monday night mass meetings were held during the protest. Following are some of the people and places:

Rev. L. Roy Bennett – South Holt St. – He was my pastor and lived in Mount Zion's parsonage.

E. D. Nixon – Clinton St. – He was a close friend of my parents, and his home was bombed. Historic Marker

Erna A. Dungee – West Jeff Davis Ave. – She was a member of our church and a friend of our family.

Attorney Fred Gray – West Jeff Davis Ave. (later Fred D. Gray Avenue.)

Thomas Gray – West Jeff Davis Ave. later Fred D. Gray Avenue – He was part-owner of Dozier's Appliance Store where we bought our first television, an Admiral console model.

Rev. Robert Gratz – Cleveland Ave. (later Rosa Parks Avenue). He was Pastor of Trinity Lutheran Church The parsonage where he and his family lived was bombed. Historic Marker

Rosa Parks – She and her husband lived in the Cleveland Avenue Apartments - Historic Marker

Rev. H. H. Hubbard – Mobile Rd. He was the Pastor of Bethel Baptist Church. Historic Marker

Rev. J. W. Bonner – Glass St. – He was our neighbor and Pastor of First C.M.E. Church that stood on the corner of Glass and Holt Streets. Glass Street and the church were obliterated by the construction of Interstate Highways 65 and 85.

Charlie and Lucille Times Home – South Holt St. – Historic Marker

Jimmie Lowe – Cleveland Ave. – She owned an adult school near our home, and her daughter, Jean was on my mother's faculty at North Highland Elementary.

Olivia Boyd – South Holt St. – She was a member of our church and friend of my family.

Eddie Posey - Early St. – His son, Eddie and I were classmates at Saint Jude. Our YMCA summer camp would meet in a building and parking lot he owned on Monroe Street.

Day Street Baptist Church – Day St. – Historic Marker

Lilly Missionary Baptist Church – Hill Street – Historic Marker

The Sherman W. White Home – West Jeff Davis Ave. – Historic Marker – Sherman White was a Tuskegee Airman.

While attending Saint Jude, I became interested in music. In the sixth grade, Sister Mary Grace who had a most angelic soprano voice allowed me to sing in the choir on Sundays when I was not serving as an altar boy. I was allowed to perform these tasks even though I was not Roman Catholic; I continued to hold my membership at Mount Zion A.M.E. Zion Church. It was under her guidance that I learned to perform Gregorian chant.

My interest in music continued and I began to explore playing musical instruments when Alabama State College Laboratory High School allowed Saint Jude students to play in the band during an extended day music program. The band directors for that program were Dr. Hayes and Mr. Clarence Edmondson. Under their tutelage, I learned to play the clarinet. After a time, I felt that I was too big physically to play such a small instrument in the marching band, so I learned to play the baritone saxophone. I had to labor assiduously to carry that big thing while marching. I looked forward to concert season so that I could play the clarinet again.

My interest in playing a musical instrument began to wane when football and basketball became more attractive. My 9th grade Algebra teacher Coach Orlando Massey was quite persuasive in encouraging me to get involved in athletics at Saint Jude where I lettered in basketball my junior and senior years.

At St. Jude we were taught that God calls individuals to a life of service, and that it is that calling that would give purpose to our lives. There I was introduced to the word vocation which is derived from the Latin term voco which means to call. To highlight the experience of being called, in our tenth-grade year, our class went on a retreat to the Dominican Monastery of St. Jude in Marbury, Alabama. It was at that retreat that all students participating were to pray and begin to listen for God's calling. This experience was an exercise in faith. Most of that day was spent in silent reflection as we walked along pathways beneath towering pine trees, and across red clay fields that were bordered by hillsides covered by kudzu vines.

Like the nuns who were cloistered behind the walls of that place, sacrifice was required; therefore, no one in our group was allowed to talk to others while we were on that fieldtrip. Following Mass, we boarded the bus for the return trip to Montgomery. It would be several years later that I would come to understand the benefits of that encounter. From a career point of view, I had no idea what I wanted to become, but I spent the remainder of my time at Saint Jude High School exploring.

In my junior year, I also became interested in histrionics and began acting in stage plays under the instruction of Miss Joan Thiele who was assisted by her friend, Mary Jo Kopechne, a Caldwell College graduate. The role I most enjoyed playing was Michael, the archangel in the play Who Donit? by C. B. Gilford. It was the first play performed on the stage of the new gymnasium at Saint Jude in 1963. Billy Phillips, a senior who played Alexander Arlington and I would later be roommates at Tuskegee. Miss Kopechne would later die in an automobile accident on Chappaquiddick Island near Martha's Vineyard, Massachusetts. The car in which the accident occurred was driven by Senator Edward Kennedy.

My interest in vocal music was revived when Mrs. Mamie Shultz, the wife of the pastor of Mount Zion A.M.E. Zion Church, invited me to become a member of the Youth Choir. She and her music ministry would have a profound impact on my life. Under her guidance, my

Saturdays became totally consumed by her demanding leadership style. From early Saturday mornings until late afternoons, we would rehearse in preparation for Sunday morning services, mass meetings, and concerts. It was during that time that I would sing my first vocal solo at Mount Zion. The selected music was "Are Ye Able,' Said the Master" by Earl Marlatt.

In the spring of 1963, I, and some of the members of the choir attended a concert at the Houston Hill Junior High School Auditorium where the Tuskegee Institute Choir was featured. I was captivated by every song that they sang: however, it was their performance of Negro Spirituals that mesmerized me. When they sang "Ezekiel Saw the Wheel" by William Dawson, I was hooked by the "Du ma lum mas." I knew then that like my father, I would have to become a member of that wonderful choir. When I got home, I told Momma and Daddy that I wanted to matriculate at Tuskegee Institute. They were quite pleased with my decision.

I applied for admission to Tuskegee and on my birthday April 10, 1964, I received an unexpected gift in the form of a letter of acceptance. I wanted to complete my undergraduate degree in three years; therefore, I had requested admission for the summer term. In his letter of acceptance Admissions Officer, Roland Henry, Jr. declared: "After due deliberation of your stated desire to enroll at Tuskegee Institute in June (even in light of the fact that past experiences indicate students enrolling under these circumstances have performed poorly during this period, and that you will not reap the benefit of the organized orientation activities made available in September to first-time entering students prior to registration), we will respect your judgment and permit you to enroll ..." That was one of the best decisions that I would ever make. What Mr. Henry did not understand was that I was in love with Freda, and I was in a hurry to get my college degree so that she and I could get married.

I wanted to be a music major but would later learn that notwithstanding the fact that Tuskegee had an outstanding band and choir; it did not have a formal baccalaureate music program. My second choice of a major was the School of Education. I had been greatly influenced by Sister Rose Marie, Helen Kolenbush, Joan Thiele, and of course Momma and Daddy. With that thought in mind, I was led by the Spirit of God to declare Education as my undergraduate major in the fields of English and social studies. Music would become a very important avocation.

I made my desires known, and on April 20, of 1964, I received a letter from Dr. William A. Hunter, Dean of the School of Education, in which he stated the following: "We are delighted to know that you have been accepted as a student to attend Tuskegee Institute and that you intend to pursue your professional teaching training in the Tuskegee Institute School of Education."

In 1964, I was given the opportunity to participate in a talent show that was sponsored by the Montgomery County Extension Office. The event took place at the Tullibody Auditorium on the campus of Alabama State Teachers College. I sang "The Holy City" by Stephen Adams. My accompanist was Jacquelyn Young who also played for the Youth Choir at Mount Zion. By the grace of God, the judges declared that I was the winner. I was presented a trophy by Mr. Robert Jones and selected to represent Montgomery County in the state-wide talent show which would be held at Tuskegee that summer.

The contest was held on the Stage of Logan Hall on the campus of Tuskegee. The audience in attendance was much larger and more raucous than that at Tullibody. The music that I selected to sing was "I'll Walk with God" from The Student Prince by Nicholas Brodzsky. When I began to sing, a hush came over the audience. Suddenly a small group in the balcony began to boo. I turned toward them and sang to them directly, and they became quiet. Upon completion of that solo, I received a standing ovation and won the contest. That solo performance gave me the confidence I needed as a beginning student at Tuskegee.

It was good that I had enrolled into the summer program when there were fewer students on campus and not many distractions that were sure to come in the fall. My dormitory experience began in Residence Hall A. Billy Phillips who was also a St. Jude graduate from the class of 1963 and I were roommates that summer. It was great sharing a room with someone I knew and trusted. With settling into our abode behind, the next challenge was learning to find my way around campus. That was a daunting task in the beginning.

The dormitories for men were located on the west side of the sprawling 5,000-acre campus. Most of my academic and social experiences would take place on the east side of the campus, an area lovingly called "the Yard." Tompkins Hall contained the dining hall and student union. Many hours were spent studying in the Hollis Burke Frissell Library - this building was named for my grandfather's mentor at Hampton. Most of my academic classes were housed in Huntingdon Hall. I also spent a lot of time toiling in Carnegie Hall during choir rehearsals.

To get to the Yard daily from my dormitories, I had to travel through the Valley during all kinds of weather. About this area, students would recite: "Down, down, down in the valley so low, five minutes and one mile to go!"[19] This space was one of the most beautiful areas on campus especially in the spring and fall when the foliage was most splendidly attired. Over time however, my goal had become to get out of the Valley. As I look back, the landmark became a metaphor for my future challenges. This idea is wonderfully reflected in the first verse of "It's in The Valleys I Grow" by Janet Eggleston which declares:

"Sometimes life seems hard to bear
Full of sorrow, trouble, and woe.
It's then I have to remember,
That it's in the valleys I grow."

Not only was the Valley a major thoroughfare for navigating the campus, but it was also in a portion of this space where the clay was excavated by students for use in making bricks. Under the leadership of Booker T. Washington, many of the original buildings at Tuskegee were constructed with resources from this area.

While managing a very rigorous academic schedule, I was able to enjoy participating in student life. When I left Montgomery, a very good friend had encouraged me to join Kappa Alpha Psi, and that was my

[19] Tuskegee Institute, Tuskeana, 1965, p. 82, Tuskegee Institute: Graduating Class of 1965, Print Archives, Hollis Burke Frissell Library.

intention until I attended my first homecoming parade in 1964. All the pageantry and excitement were a part of the festivities. My friends Billy Phillips and Palmer Sullens had joined me on the parade route which snaked through the campus past the Oaks, which had been the on-campus residence of Tuskegee Institute founder Booker T. Washington.

As the procession passed us, I observed that the members of Alpha Phi Alpha had members of that organization and their queen riding in a convertible yellow and black 1963 Ford Mustang. The Kappas and their queen drove by in a convertible red and white Chevrolet Super Sport. In the distance, I heard the cadenced drumbeat and as I looked in the direction from which that sound emanated, I could see the model of a Greek war boat being drawn by members of the Omega Psi Phi Lampados Club. Inside the boat, were members of the fraternity standing in honor of their queen. They were all sartorially resplendent in purple and gold costumes that depicted ancient Greek attire. On that spot, I decided that I would one day become a member of Omega Psi Phi Fraternity. In April of 1965, that became a reality. I pledged myself to the Omega Psi Phi Fraternity. The pledge period was long and rigorous, and my grades took a nosedive during that grueling experience. Through perseverance, scholarship, the support of caring HBCU instructors, and the grace of God, I was able to recover.

Freda, who had pledged Alpha Kappa Alpha Sorority was attending Alabama State College, and by matriculating during the summer sessions, she was on a fast track to graduation. We continued dating on weekends when I could find a ride to Montgomery. Our relationship became long-distance after her graduation on August 17, 1965, when she accepted her first teaching position at Eureka High School, a first-through-twelfth-grade school in Ashburn, Georgia. Eureka was the only educational institution for black students in a segregated Turner County, Georgia. Periodically she would ride the Greyhound Bus Line back to Montgomery, and I would make arrangements to come home so that we could keep our love alive. After all, she was still "My Girl" as my favorite song of that period by the Temptations declared.

In the 1964 Edition of the <u>Tuskeana,</u> Freda wrote the following note to me:

"Dear Peter,

Please continue striving hard for what you want and someday, you will be a great success. I hope you will never forget me or all of the nice times we've had together. May our love grow stronger each day. Peter, I will forever love you. So please stay as nice, friendly and sweet as you are now, and the best will always come to you.

I love you.

Freda"

At the end of our weekend rendezvous, I would rise early on Sunday mornings, and Daddy would drive me back to campus. The route that we would take was the Atlanta Highway (Alabama Highway 80 East). In the spring of the year, I can remember traveling through the McLemore Plantation where as far as I could see on both sides of the highway, cotton was in full bloom. Having brought my choir robe home with me, Daddy was able to take me directly Logan Hall in time for me to do my vocal warm-ups with the choir in preparation for chapel services.

The main purpose of the Tuskegee Institute Choir was to perform for Institute religious services. During my period of participation (1964-1967) under the direction of Dr. Relford Patterson, the choir also participated in the Tuskegee-Michigan Cultural Exchange Program, which included concert tours of mid-western states. In 1965, we also made two concert tours to New York City, New York. During the Fall Tour, we performed at the Waldorf Astoria Hotel where Mayor Lindsey was in attendance. In the spring, we returned to perform at Town Hall. Those concert tour were primarily Institute fund-raising activities. They also helped with student recruitment; I am a prime example of that.

The Tuskegee Institute Choir 1964 – Charles P. Everett, IV,
back row, and 1st from right side.

The order of service for Chapel was the following: Prelude, the singing of "Cast Thy Burden Upon the Lord" by Felix Mendelssohn, Prayer, Selected Music by the Institute Choir, the Sermon by the Chaplain, Offertory, Announcements, and the Benediction. All freshmen and sophomores were required to be in attendance.

When Daddy attended Tuskegee, Chapel services were held in the Institute Chapel, a building which was destroyed by fire circa 1955 and replaced by a new edifice in 1969. During the period I was there, those services and most other concerts and lectures were held in Logan Hall. Performing on that stage in 1964-65 were the following:

The Don Shirley Trio; Abbey Simon, pianist; The American Ballet Theater; Adele Addison, mezzo soprano; Ruggiero Ricci, violin virtuoso; New York Pro Musica Concert Ensemble; Miriam Makeba, folk singer; and the University of Michigan Symphony Orchestra. Among those who lectured from that stage that year included James Farmer and Malcolm X.

In addition to the venue for the events mentioned above, Logan Hall also served as a physical education and competitive sports arena for the Institute basketball and swim teams. I attended many dances in that old building. Athletes who participated in the Institute-Work-Study program would earn money for tuition and books by preparing the facility for whatever programs would be occurring there.

By attending year-round, I was able to complete the required course of study in three years. The last semester was the most challenging because I carried twenty-one semester hours including intern teaching at Tuskegee Institute High School; however, I was blessed to earn a place on the Dean's List and graduate at the age of twenty. I was also blessed to have as a supervising teacher of intern students, Mrs. Mary Ann Jones. I was inspired by her classroom-management style. I remember much of what she said as she taught her students, but what I remember most, is how she said it. To me she seemed to exude confidence, and she was always well prepared for instruction. While she was firm with her students as it related to deportment, she was also approachable. She communicated a since of high expectation, and rigor was evident in her approach to instruction.

As my family and I were leaving the Tuskegee Campus following the graduation ceremony, the last memory that I had of that day was looking back at the statue of Booker T. Washington "Lifting the Veil" by Charles Keck. I was appreciative that "long striving mother Tuskegee had lifted the veil from this diligent son, and that it would be my task to be a lifelong learner and continue to lift the veil from the heads of all the students whom I would have the honor of serving.

When I returned home, the construction of I-65 and I-85 decimated the northeastern section of the Peacock Tract, my childhood neighborhood. Because no on-or-off ramps were built, the neighborhood began to die. This caused the Montgomery diaspora, an event scattering the residence of the community and negatively impacting commerce. All the businesses that were in the neighborhood moved. Because of the dearth of grocery stores and cafes, the area became a food desert. Momma and Daddy sold our home on Glass Street and moved to the Westwood Estates in the southwest section of Montgomery. Other neighbors and Mount Zion members who were forced to move were Mrs. Julia Mae Phelps from Chilton Street to Doris Circle in the Ridgecrest community. Mr. Ozel Jackson and family from Chilton Street to Goode Street (now E. D. Nixon Street). The Mount Zion parsonage where pastors and civil rights leaders L. Roy Bennett, S. S. Seay, Percy Smith, Jr. had resided was demolished. Because of those conditions, the Church's membership moved to another campus on West Jeff Davis Avenue (now Fred D. Gray Avenue) in 1990.

Other churches that played leadership roles in the 20th-Century-Civil- Rights Movement were also negatively impacted. First C. M. E. Church that stood at the corner of Glass and Holt Streets was demolished and the members moved to a building on Oak Street in Ridgecrest. The Metropolitan M. E. Church was torn down, and members moved to an edifice on Cleveland Avenue. Beulah Baptist Church was destroyed, and members moved to a building on Cleveland Avenue (now Rosa Parks) in Ridgecrest. Maggie Street Baptist Church moved to Grove Street. All those buildings had stood directly in the path of I – 85.

Interstate and Memorial Annex - 1990

I had rushed my college training at Tuskegee, earning a diploma in three years. Before I began teaching, there was something much more important that had to do. After all, it had caused the rush. I was in love with Alfredia Brown, and we had been engaged for two years. On June 11, 1967, the Sunday following my graduation, Alfredia became my bride.

The wedding took place at Mount Zion A.M.E. Zion Church where Reverend Percy Smith, Jr. officiated. The ceremony was forty-five minutes late starting. The church was packed on that warm Sunday afternoon. John Sawyer, Sr. accompanied by Gwen Liggon performed pre-nuptial music. My soul was lifted as I listened to "O Promise", "Because" and other traditional wedding music. As Alfredia entered escorted by her father, I cold see her dark lovely eyes from behind her veil, and the words: "hearing Gods message while the organ rolls its mighty music to our very souls; no love more perfect that a life with thee. "O promise me, o promise me" echoed to my very core.

In September of 1967, I fulfilled my calling by launching out into a world that had gone crazy. American cities had erupted into protests because of the Vietnam Conflict. Many of America's youth had lost their minds that had been spaced out by LSD (lysergic acid diethylamide); they were a part of the hippy culture. "Black Power" had become the mantra of the Black Panther Party, and an organization that had been formed not far away in neighboring Lowndes County. George Wallace was leading a reborn conservative movement and his wife Lurlene had replaced him as Governor of Alabama. It was against this backdrop that I would get my professional start.

My teaching career, ironically, began at Marbury High School where my father's would end. I was hired in 1967 by the Autauga County Board of Education when Mr. John R. Hargis was Superintendent to be one of the teachers who would fulfill Judge Frank Johnson's Court Order to desegregate the instructional staffs of Autauga County. Daddy retired 1976 as the first African American Guidance Counselor at Marbury High School. It perhaps seems strange that a son would blaze the trail for his father. This was the case for me and Daddy.

This school was in the northwest corner of Autauga County and 29.5 miles from Montgomery, Alabama via US-31 north. Although other schools in that county had desegregated student enrollment since the 1966-67 School Year, Marbury had no Black students enrolled. Jacquelyn Warren Jones and I would be the first African Americans to enter the classrooms there. I was assigned to teach history in grades seven through eleven and one physical education class. Jacquelyn was assigned six business education classes.

Alfredia was assigned to teach physical education at Prattville Junior High School in Prattville, Alabama. Other Black teachers serving with her were Annie Pearle Rudolph and Philip Steele.

As the first day of school approached, I was fearful for two reasons. Firstly, this would be my first-year teaching solo as a new instructor. Secondly, although I had attended Saint Jude and had White teachers, I had never taught White students. Thirdly, the fear of the unknown loomed large. What would be the response of the White community to our coming? Would the transition be peaceful or violent? Not having the answers to these questions made for restless nights; however, we gained comfort by knowing that Black children had already blazed the trail at Prattville Junior High and at Autauga County High School and at schools in Montgomery where they began the process of desegregation in 1965. In addition, there were other blacks and whites who were carrying out Judge Johnson's decree. Momma was the principal of North Highland Elementary and the two White teachers would be blazing the trail there.

We had concluded that we were not alone, for we believed that God was with us, and we needed the money; there would be no turning back. Since the patriarch escaped enslavement, the mission of the Everett family has been to find the route to life, liberty, and the pursuit of happiness through education. This includes encouraging others to follow us down that path.

The morning of the first day of school that year, I drove our 1966 gold GTO into the parking lot of Prattville Junior High where Freda nervously yet courageously got out and walked through the crowd of students who stared at her in awe and amazement as she walked through the doors of the red brick one story structure. She would tell me later that one student was so resentful of her being there that he held his nose as she passed, shouted "nigger" and fell over into a nearby trash can. This of course drew laughter from his friends. Freda indicated that other than that one negative event, she was apprehensively accepted by the students, faculty, and administrative staff.

Jacquelyn, who rode with me each morning, and I traveled northwestward on the undulating and curvaceous US-31w to the small community of Marbury. That morning, we drove most of the way behind a yellow school bus out of which the student passengers stared at us with cold and questioning gazes. Suddenly, I recognized a sign to my left which read, the Dominican Monastery of St. Jude. I had experienced an epiphany. What I was about to do that morning was the beginning of God's calling me into service as a professional educator.

As we listened to "Love is Blue" by Paul Mauriat and his Orchestra on the radio, the school building came into view. We entered the tree lined campus and parked in front of the burgundy-colored brick building that was trimmed in white. Wearing a brown business suit, shirt, and tie, I grabbed my brown attaché case got out of the car and along with Jacquelyn, climbed the steps which led to two center doors.

Mr. Woodfin, the principal, was standing by the door of his office. He greeted us warmly as we approached him. I proceeded to my classroom which was located around the corner from the administrative office. It was comforting knowing that help was in proximity should I need it.

When my first period of instruction began, it must have been strange for the students to see my standing in front of the classroom dressed professionally. The outfit that I wore was accompanied by the confident look that appeared on my visage. That was something I had learned from Mrs. Mary Ann Jones who had supervised my student teaching at Tuskegee Institute High School. She always wore confidence on her countenance. The typical attire for the male teachers at Marbury High School was a plaid shirt, dress paints, black shoes with white socks. The only other Black male that the students may have observed was the Coca Cola delivery man who wore a camel-colored outfit with green stripes which distinguished him from the White delivery man's uniform which was white with green stripes.

That first year, Marbury was not accredited by the Southern Association of Colleges and Schools; therefore, the Autauga County School system did not have mandatory limits on important things like number of instructional preparations and class size. I had been assigned six instructional preparations which included the following: 7th Grade World Geography; 8th Grade American History; 9th Grade Alabama History, 10th Grade World History; 11th Grade American History and a combined physical education class. In my suit and tie, I supervised volleyball, football, and softball; however, I did remove my jacket and loosened my tie. Quite frankly, I was overwhelmed by the challenge of delivering successful instruction facing that many preparations. Through study, perseverance, and the inspiration of the Holy Spirit, I was able to survive.

The 8th Grade American History class had the largest enrollment. There were fifty-four students in that group. As far as mental ability was concerned, the students were instructionally inclusive. I had to plan to reach the gifted, the average and the mentally challenged. By the grace of God, I succeeded by establishing an instructional routine that incorporated best practices that I had learned at Tuskegee Institute. The students felt that my teaching style was rigorous. In the 1968 copy of the yearbook of the school, the Marala, one student wrote about me the following: "To a nice history teacher, but a hard one." I believed in challenging the students to be their best selves academically.

There were daily challenges with racism. Some students came from homes where they were taught to be respectful to adults and especially to teachers. Some students reflected their being reared in an intolerant environment. To avoid calling me Mr. Everett, a few addressed me as professor in a negative sense. One young man in my 10th grade class was enamored with Adolph Hitler. A loner socially, he was constantly drawing swastikas in his notebook and on the book cover of his textbooks. During the year, I would have many one-on-one conversations with him concerning his understanding of Nazism. I always tried to point him toward what history had to say about Hitler and atrocities toward Jews vis-à-vis the Holocaust sited in the textbook. Whether or not he ever accepted the truth about Hitler is doubtful, but he had developed a respectful relationship with me as his first African American teacher. In the <u>Marala</u>, he wrote the following at the end of that academic year: "I hope you come back next year."

The most challenging experience I had that first year of desegregation occurred on April 4, 1968. As I was preparing to leave for Marbury, I observed that the morning was especially bright and sunny. Freda, who was on maternity with our first pregnancy, had not experienced any morning-sickness problems and was in a good mood that day. It appeared that this would be a beautiful spring day; but that thought was quickly shattered by my next-door neighbor and childhood friend, Albert Harris, Jr. After answering his knock at the front door, he frantically informed me that he was carrying his gun and advised me that I should get mine. When I inquired why I needed a gun, he informed me that Dr. King had been shot during the night in Memphis, Tennessee. I went back to the bedroom to deliver the awful news to Freda who was shocked about what I had reported. I finished getting dressed, Freda and I said our goodbyes, and I went off to Marbury with a heavy heart. Going to work on that occasion was very difficult for me.

When Jacquelyn and I arrived that day, we went directly to our classrooms. I did not know what to expect from the students. As I entered my classroom, I noticed that all the material that I had left neatly on my desk was now on the floor. My chair was upside-down, and the room was in general disarray. In the back of the classroom to my right, a group of the ninth graders had gathered, and they began to laugh. Suddenly, one of the young men ran up to me and breathlessly announced: "Hey Professor Everett; you've got to hide me. I shot that coon last night." I set my jaws, clenched my fists and stared deeply into his eyes. I was able to refrain from knocking the hell out of that racist young man when the words of Dr. Nebritt came to my remembrance: "Some of you in this graduating class are going to have the strength of Samson, the wisdom of Solomon, the patience of Job and the stomach of a damn billy goat to withstand some of the challenges that lie ahead. Those words kept me from falling into a trap that awaited me in that hateful situation.

I turned from him, walked over to my desk, and began to pick up the books and papers that were strewn across the floor. One of the female students who had been observing from another area in the classroom came over to me, helped me to put things back in place and whispered that she was sorry that Rev. King had been killed. For the rest of that day, I attempted to stay as close to the instructional routine as I could. I did my best to keep the youngsters on task.

One of my students from that period would call me in 2020, fifty-two years later and apologize. I was touched by his contrite spirit as he confessed; I attempted to assuage the pain of the moment by blaming his actions on his age and the time. He would have none of that and responded: "Don't try to water it down Mr. Everett. I was wrong, I was a jerk, and I am asking you to forgive me." I forgave him and continued to listen. This was my first time experiencing an individual confront his own racist past behavior. What I learned from that encounter was that the beginning of overcoming racism is to be willing to admit how wrong that type of behavior is, and to be willing to seek forgiveness from the one offended.

I continued to teach at Marbury through the 1968-69 academic year, and although, I felt I was making a positive impact there, I wanted to teach closer to Montgomery. Freda and I applied for positions there, and we were interviewed by Mr. Silas Garrett who was the assistant superintendent at that time. Mr. Walter McKee was the superintendent. I was sent to Cloverdale Junior High to meet with the principal, Mr. Edward "Ed" Richardson. The interview went well, and I received a letter from Mr. Garret dated May 30, 1969, which offered me a position to teach six periods of seventh grade Social Studies at Cloverdale Junior High School at a salary of $609.00 per month beginning on September 1, of that year. Freda was sent to Dannelly Elementary to be interviewed by Mrs. Ilene Hall who was the principal. She was also recommended for hiring and was assigned to teach fifth grade. I welcomed the idea of having only one instructional preparation and far fewer miles to travel daily.

By my second year at Cloverdale, Mr. Glen Adams was assigned to be principal, and he placed me in the position of ninth grade English teacher. After three years, I was finally teaching in my major field of study. Following a year and a semester in that position, I was asked to become the Guidance counselor of Cloverdale.

Finding a private place to meet with students was my first challenge. After looking through the building, I found a textbook storage room that was located near the administrative office that I thought would provide excellent space for the new Guidance office. After presenting a design of the office and some possible fund-raising ideas, Mr. Adams agreed and by the summer, the room was remodeled by students from the Montgomery Area Vocational School under the direction of their carpentry instructor. It was ready for occupancy by the opening of the next school year.

In the summer of 1973, Mr. Clinton Carter, Principal of Lee High School, recommended me to Mr. Walter McKee, Superintendent of the Montgomery Public School System, to become an administrative assistant there. The promotion to Lee's leadership team set in motion a process from which I was able to develop the skills necessary for guiding a school community successfully. I remained under Mr. Carter's tutelage for five years before being assigned to the Principalship of Houston Hill Junior High School.

Between 1976 and 1978, I experienced the deaths of Mrs. Betty Brown, Freda's mother and the passing away of my mother, Mrs. Minnie Everett. These two committed women gave of themselves through Christian ministry at Mount Zion A.M.E. Zion Church until the end of their earthly lives.

In 1975, Mrs. Brown's, Momma Betty as we lovingly referred to her, health began to fail. Being one who did not want to be totally dependent on others to provide her transportation, she continued to drive her white Ford Pinto even though she did not have her driver's license. At Mount Zion A.M.E. Zion Church, she served as a class leader. In that official capacity, she was responsible for checking on the spiritual and physical wellbeing of church members assigned to her care. This often required her to visit the sick in their homes. On Easter morning of 1976, Freda and I were preparing to attend worship service when we received a phone call from my mother. She told me that someone had called her and reported that Momma Betty had been involved in a car accident in front of Lilly Missionary Baptist Church on Hill Street which was located one block from where she lived on Carlisle Street.

I left Freda with the children and drove to where the accident had occurred. When I arrived, I observed her Pinto parked in front of the church, but she was not there. I inquired among those who were bystanders if they knew what had happened to the driver of the Pinto. I was told that she had been taken away in an ambulance to Baptist Hospital on the Southern Blvd.

I immediately got back into our Toyota Corona and drove to Baptist Hospital. Upon my arrival, I rushed to the emergency room where I learned that Mamma Betty was pronounced dead on arrival. The cause of death was cardiac arrest. I did not call Freda from the hospital because I wanted to be with her when I told her the bad news.

When I arrived, Freda had dressed the children, and was putting on her clothes. I walked over to her, held her tightly and told her what had happened. Needless to say, the news was not taken well. Resurrection morning was certainly a challenge for our family. But we found solace in the fact that her faith had caused her to serve until the end of her earthly life and that she had died on the battlefield helping others.

In 1978, after laboring five years at Lee High School, I had finally joined my grandfather, father and mother professionally by becoming the fourth member of my immediate family to be a school principal in Alabama. In a letter dated May 25, 1978, Mr. H. H. Adair, Associate Superintendent, confirmed my appointment as principal of Houston Hill Junior High School for the school year beginning July 1, 1978, for 12 months per year beginning at a salary rate of $17,872.20. I replaced Mrs. Rose Lott who had been a friend of our family and served on my father's staff at North Highland High School in Prattville, Alabama.

My family and I were elated with my promotion. During the month of July that year, Aunt Elan and Uncle Eugene Smith came down from Cleveland, Ohio. My mother was so proud when I gave them a tour of the school building. This great joy would be short-lived.

Later that month, our church Mount Zion A.M.E. Zion, then located at 657 South Holt Street, sponsored a week of spiritual revival services. Momma, even though she was declining in her physical health, volunteered to host an afternoon meal at her residence on Mobile Drive in Westwood Estates on July 25. She had been in bed most of the morning with an excruciating headache but got up to attend to details. Shortly after 3o'clock p.m., the guests arrived. Those attending were the guest revival evangelist, our pastor, Reverend Lloyd Burton, his family and his preacher's steward, Mr. Mosley Murray, Sr. Freda, I and our children, and my brother Ronnie's wife Cheryl and their children. My father and my cousins Eloise Lewis and Ora Bell Smith were in the kitchen helping prepare the meal.

We were engaged in lively conversation and a discussion of scripture which led Momma to quote from Isaiah 35:8. She then walked from the dining room where the adults were eating to the den where the children were enjoying their meal. It was there where she suffered a cerebral hemorrhage. We attempted to revive her while waiting for the ambulance to arrive. The preachers prayed fervently over her body. All attempts at revival failed. When the paramedics arrived, they did all they could to no avail. Like Momma Betty, she died on the battlefield of service to our Lord and Savior Jesus the Christ.

In August, Mrs. Annie S. Thomas, who was serving as superintendent of the Sunday school at Mount Zion told me that she was interested in starting a class for college students and young professionals. She asked me to become a Sunday school teacher for that group. At that difficult time, that was the last thing I wanted to do, but Sister Thomas was able to convince me to take on that challenge. When I told Alfredia that I had accepted the position, she said that she would be my first student. Sister Thomas is responsible for the great joy that I get out of serving in ministry. She would often tell me to trust in God, and He would be a light unto my path. That certainly has proven true for me, and it helped me overcome my grieving following Momma's passing away.

Though challenging, that first year at Houston Hill was great success. Alfredia celebrated by presenting me a gold-plated paperweight for my office desk. Hidden behind her gift was a reminder of a lesson I had taught as a new Sunday school teacher. The lesson was based on Ephesians 5:22-25 (New International Version) which states:

22Wives, submit yourselves to your own husbands as you do to the Lord. **23**For the husband is the head of the wife as Christ is the head of the church, his body, of which he is the Savior. **24**Now as the church submits to Christ, so also wives should submit to their husbands in everything.

25Husbands, love your wives, just as Christ loved the church and gave himself up for her **26**to make her holy, cleansing her by the washing with water through the word, **27**and to present her to himself as a radiant church, without stain or wrinkle or any other blemish, but holy and blameless. **28**In this same way, husbands ought to love their wives as their own bodies. He who loves his wife loves himself. **29**After all, no one ever hated their own body, but they feed and care for their body, just as Christ does the church— **30**for we are members of his body. **31**"For this reason a man will leave his father and mother and be united to his wife, and the two will become one flesh." ᶠ **32**This is a profound mystery—but I am talking about Christ and the church. **33**However, each one of you also must love his wife as he loves himself, and the wife must respect her husband.

Not having a good understanding of this passage, I would remind Alfredia that I am the head of the wife and there were certain things that I expected her to do for me. After a time, she had gotten tired of my being the boss. She looked at me one day and said: "Let me tell you something! You may be the head, but I'm the neck, and I will turn you any way I want to." After that reply, I sought to gain a better understanding of Ephesians 5. As a husband and school principal, I learned to work toward becoming a servant-leader rather than a boss-leader.

My learning to become a servant-leader is reflected in the following letter from one of my white military parent's view of my first year.

At Houston Hill, I was able to spread my wings and provide the kind of leadership that caused excitement around teaching and learning. I believed that a principal should be highly visible; therefore, I would daily visit every classroom after I had made morning announcements. I would not allow myself to get trapped in my office behind a desk. My being out communicated to the teachers and students that we were all in this educational endeavor together and that if the faculty and staff needed me, I was available to them. If a parent came for a conference, when possible, I would have the conversation with that individual while walking through the building. This allowed the parent to get a sense of a safe and orderly school where instruction was taking place in a happy and structured environment.

During the walk through the building, parents not only saw teachers providing excellent instruction, but they saw the custodial staff at work cleaning the building. I would take them into the restrooms to show that our walls were free of graffiti and gang symbols. During our walk, if I saw paper on the floor in the corridors, I would stop and pick it up. In the end, most parents enjoyed the experience.

By January of my fifth year at Houston Hill, parents and teachers honored my service by nominating me for the "Outstanding Principal Award." Following is the letter of nomination from PTA members Gene and Polly Fehler dated January 27, 1983:

"Mr. Charles P. Everett, principal of Houston Hill Junior High School for the past five years, is an extraordinary nominee for Outstanding Principal Award. As PTA officers and parents of two Houston Hill students, we have had the privilege of observing directly the positive effects of Mr. Everett's enthusiastic, innovative, and caring approach to education.

Through Mr. Everett's strong leadership, Houston Hill's students and parents have joined in a cooperative effort to show how learning and growth need not be limited to traditional classroom and athletic activities. Mr. Everett's establishment of an annual Fine Arts Festival has given students the opportunity to demonstrate their talents in art, music and drama in presentations that can be shared by not only the student body, but by the community at large. His involvement with Houston Hill's sponsorship of an annual Donkey Ball game and his creation of the Festival on the Hill (annual "carnival" and rummage sale) have brought students, parents and teachers together in fun-filled fund-raising experiences.

Of particular significance is Mr. Everett's administration of Houston Hill's Academic Pep Rally, which demonstrates that success in academics deserves the type of assembly program and cheering section usually reserved for athletics. In the Academic Pep Rally, parents and students join together in the school gymnasium to cheer for competing math teams. As the team goes to the center of the court for the start of the contest, cheerleaders lead the gathered assembly in cheers for the academic participants. Students learn that their strong academic performance is something to be strived for, and that it will be recognized in a positive way. Every homeroom class a Houston Hill uses part of its time each morning to work on math problems to assure that each student has increased opportunities to eliminate problem areas in math and to achieve at a higher level.

As a fund raiser, Mr. Everett exerts untiring efforts to help the school earn additional funds for air conditioning so that the students might have conditions more amenable to learning. Above all, his primary concern is for the welfare of his students. He is consistent and firm in his belief that each student has tremendous personal worth, and that the school's learning climate provides the chance for each student's potential to be realized if the student is willing to put forth the effort. His constant message to his students is that they are able to say, 'I am somebody,' and that they are not afraid to strive for academic excellence. He is also a believer in the need for strong discipline. Under his direction, Houston Hill's disciplinary problems have been in steady decline, leading to corresponding improvement in academic performance.

Mr. Everett has solicited, encouraged, and gained the support of many parents who willingly volunteer their time and talents at Houston Hill during the school day. Parents work in the school library, in the offices, and even in the classrooms to share their various areas of expertise. Mr. Everett's thoughtful acknowledgement of the efforts of the volunteers has had tremendous positive benefits for not only the school's programs, but for the morale of the volunteers.

In PTA meetings, committee meetings, and in his daily duties at Houston Hill, Mr. Everett encourages parents and students to meet with him and to share with him their concerns and their suggestions. His enthusiasm, optimism and conscious attention to the needs and problems of students, parents, and teachers is commendable. That so many of Houston Hill's students are graduating with both the necessary preparation to meet the challenges of high school and with a personal sense of worth is in no small way attributable to Mr. Everett's caring leadership.

Because of Mr. Everett's sincere concern for his students and because of his commitment to his responsibilities as principal of Houston Hill Junior High School, we feel that he is an exceptionally deserving nominee for the Outstanding Principal's Award."

By the grace of God not only did I receive "Outstanding Secondary School Principal," but Houston Hill was awarded the "Community Service Award" and tied for the "Best Overall School in Montgomery County." The headline in the Wednesday, February 27, 1985, Edition of the <u>Montgomery Advertiser</u>, read, "Houston Hill Captures Three Awards."

At the end of that school year, I was transferred to the position of assistant principal of Carver Senior High School where Dwight Madison was principal. Yolanda my oldest child also joined me there as a student during her senior year of high school. Yolanda had a keen interest in radio and television broadcasting as a future vocation. While there, she participated in the outstanding magnet school program named the Carver Performing Arts Center (CPAC). Earlene Hollinger was her magnet school instructor. Although working again at the high school level was fulfilling, I enjoyed working with junior high/middle school students more. When Lewis Grayson, principal of Carver Junior High announced his retirement, I applied for that position and was assigned principal there for the 1988-89 school year.

With that appointment, Bro. Rabbit had been thrown back into the briar patch. I was free again to experiment with administrative leadership in my style. I began by building a new instructional staff which I led toward focusing instructionally on student learning following the middle school concept. This proved quite a challenge in a system that continued to follow the 7-9 grade configuration and viewed junior high as a "little high school" where departmentalizing the subjects was stressed. Helping teachers learn to work in teams also proved to be a challenge, but in time became a morale buster when they began to transition to the new approach to instruction, working together to support each other, students, and parents. When we learned to work together in small teaching communities the buy-in was overwhelming. The instructional program changes were supported by an extended-day program which we named the "Success Express." When students needed extra support with their core subjects, they were able to receive it for an additional hour after the traditional school day ended.

Discipline problems were resolved in "Saturday School." Certain rule violations could have resulted in students being suspended from school. Parents and students had the freedom to choose suspension or coming to school for three hours on Saturday morning. Parents had to sign the students in at 9:00 a.m. and sign them out at 12:00 p.m. Students would participate in counseling, physical and other motivational activities. Funding for the "Success Express" and "Saturday School" Programs came from Montgomery City Councilman Joseph Dickerson's Discretionary Fund.

About my instructional leadership, one of my white colleagues who was also principal of a westside Montgomery junior high school, described it as ethereal in nature. Although he was being whimsical in his observation, I have no doubt that God had ordered my path. This was affirmed during one of the most challenging times that I experienced at Carver Junior High when mysteriously some of my female teachers began having money stolen from their purses. Even after reporting these theft incidents to the police and having them to investigate, there did not seem to be an end to that problem in sight.

One day, at my wits end, I prayed to God and asked to open my eyes to what was causing the thefts. I wanted him to open my eyes as he had done for Hagar in Genesis 21:19 which declares: "Then God opened her eyes and she saw a well of water. She went and filled the skin with water; and gave the boy a drink." A week after that prayer, while I was sitting at my desk in my office toiling over a mundane school issue, my secretary escorted a female student into the room, and told me that the child was having trouble with her locker. I told the girl to have a seat and that I would help her shortly. After quickly completing my task. I stood pulled a copy of my locker combination book from a desk drawer and asked the student to take me to her locker so that we could determine what the problem could be.

She led me to the second floor of the ninth-grade wing of the building. After arriving, I began assisting her with the locker problem. While working with the lock, I noticed a security guard enter the corridor from the back stairwell. He crossed in front of us without noticing our presence. As he did, he took a key from his pocket, inserted it into a classroom door, and entered the room. Something told me to follow him to see what he was doing. As I entered the room, I observed his rummaging through a purse that the teacher had left in her desk drawer. He still did not notice my presence, but I continued to observe his actions. Finally, I asked him why he was going through the teacher's purse? Shocked and frightened, he fumbled the pocketbook onto the floor scattering the contents. God had answered my prayer by opening my eyes to the theft problem.

I escorted the security guard to my office and asked my secretary to call the police. I cannot recall what happened to the girl whom I was assisting, and she never came back to me for help with her locker. All that I can say is that God works in mysterious and miraculous ways. Ethereal? One can call it what one will; I call it being aligned with God's permissive will.

In addition to ordering my steps during my vocational journey, He had also placed parents and grandparents in that path from whom I had learned. He had placed Dr. Barksdale my personal physician, in my path to share ideas with me about leadership. I had a wife who reminded me that bossy-top- down leadership was not an effective style for guiding an organization including a family. Servant leadership is key. Jesus reminds us that anybody can be great if he or she is a servant first. After my learning experience at Carver Junior High School, I was selected by Superintendent Pete Eberheart to become Director of Magnet School programs, and later Executive Assistant to the Superintendent of Montgomery Public Schools. In 1999, Dr. Ed Richardson, Alabama State Superintendent of Education selected me to be a member of a team of Chief Academic Officers to guide school improvement in Alabama. From 1999 to 2004, I was assigned to Barbour, Bullock,

Lowndes, Macon, Montgomery, and Russell Counties to help with school improvement.

Another highpoint in my educational experience occurred in May of 2000 when I was invited to Tuskegee University by Dr. Mary Ann Jones, Dean of the College of Liberal Arts and Education to be the guest speaker for the Annual Senior Induction Ceremony of education graduates. The emphasis of my presentation was to communicate that they had chosen a respected career that would make a tremendous impact on generations to come. I stressed that one of the most challenging things about teaching was the four-way agenda they must balance which includes the following: student characteristics, teaching strategies, subject matter, and the personal dimension which includes their attitude toward learning.[20] I closed my speech by reciting a poem by Ivan Fitzwater titled "Only A Teacher." The last verse asks: "Only a teacher? Thank God I have a calling to the greatest profession of all! I must be vigilant every day lest I lose one fragile opportunity to improve tomorrow."

---

[20] Norman A. Sprinthall, Richard C. Sprinthall, and Shaon N. Oja, Educational Psychology A Developmental Approach, p. 7, (New York: Published by McGraw-Hill, Inc., (1994).

CHAPTER 6

THE NEXT GENERATION

In 2005, I was called out of retirement by the Montgomery County Board of Education to become the interim principal of Georgia Washington Middle School. The circle had been completed, for this was where Charles P. Everett, Jr. had begun our family's educational journey in Alabama in 1896. This was the apotheosis of my career in education. I thought this had crowned my task as an educator; however, in 2013, I was called out of retirement again to become interim principal of Georgia Washington Middle School. This time, my grandson James Thomas Cummings, III was enrolled there as an eighth-grade student.

It has been said that the fruit does not fall far from the tree, and so it is with my children. Yolanda is now a teacher of gifted students at Fickett Elementary School in Atlanta, Georgia. She is the mother of Daija, a 10th-grade honor student. Charles P. Everett, V teaches fifth grade students at Fickett Elementary. His older child, Latrice is a graduate of The Ohio State University where she earned Bachelor of Science and Master of Science degrees in social work. She is currently a social worker in the school system of Columbus, Ohio. Charles P. Everett, VI is an eighth grader at Chapel Hill Middle School. His mother is a mathematics teacher in Douglasville, Georgia at Douglas County High School. Melanie Everett Cummings is a teacher in the Montgomery County Public School System. Her son James Cummings, III and daughter, Carrington are enrolled at Trenholm Community

College of Montgomery, Alabama. I have challenged them to write the next volume of our family's journey.

As I write the final chapter of this volume, Donald John Trump has just completed one term as President of the United States of America, and Joseph Robinette Biden, Sr. has just ascended to the Presidency. A prelude to this historic event, was the eruption of the scourge of White supremacy which manifested itself on January 6, 2021, when at the urging of the outgoing President, violent insurrectionists stormed and breached the United States Capitol. The last time that edifice was breached took place during the War of 1812 by a foreign adversary. This bloody event, in which five died, was followed by Donald Trump's refusal to attend the Inauguration Ceremony of his successor. The last time that happened was in 1869, when outgoing President Andrew Johnson refused to attend the Inauguration of Ulysses S. Grant. The unfortunate similarity between Johnson and Trump was that the former was the first President to be impeached and the latter, the first to be impeached twice.

As I reflect on this unfortunate situation, two words emerge as salient. The first is erosion. As a child who grew up on an unpaved Glass Street, I observed that after a torrential rainstorm, the soil on the hill in front of some homes would be washed away. What happened to our family after the reconstruction of the South eroded the civil rights that had been gained because of the 14th Amendment to the Constitution of the United States. Segregation and disenfranchisement are just two examples of that erosion. Today, there is a concerted effort in some states to make it more difficult to vote, thus eroding the progress of our journey in civil rights.

The second word is healing. At this juncture our nation stands in need of healing. I pray that the Lord raises up Joseph R. Biden, Sr. to be a healer-in-chief. As a family, we also need healing from the bitterness of what James Weldon Johnson called "the chastening rod felt in the days when hope unborn had died," by holding on to the hope that has been resurrected by the sacrifices of those who have persevered to get us to this point in our contorted journey. We celebrate the strides that have been made, while realizing that life in the promised land is not bereft of challenges. Remaining free in a place that is becoming a more perfect Union is a never-ending effort, and there are those who seek to impede our progress. With this thought in mind, let us march on; let us climb higher; and let us do our part to make the United States of America a more perfect place to flourish. Finally, let us keep this hope alive by trusting in the God of our fathers and mothers, in the name of His Son, Jesus, the Christ.

CHAPTER 7

THE GENEOLOGY OF THE EVERETT FAMILY

Family Tree

The Everett's Branch

Slave Owners – Isaac Patterson of Caswell County, North Carolina 1792

John Everett of Caswell County, North Carolina 1767-1858

First Generation

Charles Paterson Everett, Sr. 5/4/1830 - 6/2/1909   Mary Ann Wiggins (Everett)

North Carolina   North Carolina

Children:

Nancy E. - 1867

Louisa H. - 1866

Charles P., Jr. - 1870

Mary A. - 1873

John - 1874

Second Generation

Charles P. Everett, Jr. 1870-1939   Maggie Gee (Everett) 1874-1932

Norfolk, Virginia   Mount Meigs, Alabama

Child:

Charles P., III - 1912

Third Generation

Charles P. Everett, III
7/9/1912 - 12/1/1983
Mount Meigs, Alabama
Children:
Charles P., IV - 1947
Sandra J. - 1948
Ronnie -1950

Minnie Louise Smith
11/4/1914 - 7/25/1978
Hayneville, Alabama

Fourth Generation

Charles P. Everett, IV 4/10/47
Montgomery, Alabama
Children:
Yolanda L. -1968
Charles P., V - 1971
Melanie L. - 1976

Alfredia Y. Brown (Everett) 3/6/1945
Hope Hull, Alabama

Fifth Generation

Yolanda Latrice Everett (Duncan) 5/18/68
Montgomery, Alabama
St. Jude Hospital
Child:
Deija – 5/21/08

Lester Duncan – 11/17/69
Denver, Colorado

Charles P. Everett, V 11/4/70
Montgomery, Alabama
St. Marguerite Hospital
Child:
Latrice Lashaun –
Baptist Hospital South

Bonita Congleton (Everett)
New Jersey

Shanda Latrice Hill (Everett) –
7/30/72
Daytona, Florida

Child:
Charles P., VI – 8/25/08

Melanie Lashaun Everett (Cummings)   James T. Cummings, Jr.
1/10/76
Montgomery, Alabama
St. Marguerite Hospital
Children:
James T., III – 4/3/1999
Baptist Hospital South
Carrington- 1/6/2003
Baptist Hospital South

The Gee's Family Branch

The First Generation

Joseph Gee-1856   Malinda Thompson (Gee) 1856
Alabama   Tennessee
Children:
Maggie-1874
Dora-1878

The Second Generation

Maggie Lee Gee (Everett)-1874   Charles P. Everett, Jr.-1870
Mount Meigs, Alabama   Norfolk, Virginia
Child:
Charles P. Everett, III

The Third Generation

Charles P. Everett, III-7/91912
Mount Meigs, Alabama

Minnie Smith (Everett)-11/4/1914
Hayneville, Alabama

The Fourth Generation

Charles P. Everett, IV-4/10/1947

Alfredia Brown (Everett)-3/6/1945

The Smith's Family Branch

The First Generation

Martin Smith
Children:
Henry
Martin
Phillip
Bama
Mary
Julie
Melissa
Will Morgan

Bell Smith

The Second Generation

Martin Smith, Jr.
Children:
Georgia
Alice
William
Eugene
Hugh-1891

Liddie Brown (Smith)

The Third Generation

Hugh Smith-6/16/1891-5/31/1979   Sally Miles (Smith) 7/8/1894-1969
Children:
Minnie-1914
Eugene

The Fourth Generation

Minnie Smith (Everett)-   Charles P. Everett, III-
11/4/1914-7/25/1978   7/12/1912-12/1/1983
Hayneville, Alabama   Mount Meigs, Alabama
Children:
Charles P. -1947
Sandra J.-1949
Ronnie-1950

The Fifth Generation

Charles P. Everett, IV-4/10/1947   Alfredia Brown (Everett) 3/6/1945

The Freeman's Family Branch

The First Generation

Wesley Freeman   Sally Freeman
Child:
Hester

The Second Generation

Hester Freeman (Brown)   John Brown
Children:
Chester

Scott
Joe
Candas
Johnny
"Woman"
Liddie

The Third Generation

Liddie Brown (Smith)   Martin Smith

The Fourth Generation

Hugh Smith-6/16/1891   Sally Miles (Smith) 7/8/1894

The Fifth Generation

Minnie Smith (Everett)-1914   Charles P. Everett, III-1912

The Sixth Generation

Charles P. Everett, IV-1947   Alfredia Brown (Everett)-1945

The Seventh Generation

Yolanda Duncan   Charles P Everett, V   Melanie Cummings

The Eighth Generation

Latrice Everett, Charles P. Everett, VI, Daija Duncan, James Cummings, III, Carrington Cummings

The Miles's Family Branch

The First Generation

Levi Miles-1845-8/13/1913   Sallie Rudolph (Miles)-1860-1930
Children:
Levi, Jr.12/1891 – 2/26/1912
John-8/8/1875
Samuel-10/10/1880
Anna-8/6/1882
Edie-4/9/1885
Redrey-1888
Sallie-7/8/1894

The Second Generation

Sallie Miles (Smith)-7/8/1894-1969   Hugh Smith-6/16/1891
Hayneville, Alabama   Hayneville, Alabama
Children:
Minnie L.-11/4/1914
Eugene-

The Third Generation

Minnie Smith (Everett)-   Charles P. Everett, III-
11/4/1914-7/1978   7/12/1912-12/1/1983

The Fourth Generation

Charles P. Everett, IV-4/10/1947   Alfredia Y. Brown (Everett)-3/6/1945

The Rudolph's Family Branch

The First Generation

Jim Rudolph
South Carolina
Child:
Sallie-1849
Eli-1860
Burrell-1866

Chinie or Chani Rudolph
Calhoun, Alabama

The Second Generation

Sallie Rudolph (Miles) -1860– 1/21/1930
Hayneville, Alabama

Levi Miles-1845-1913

The Third Generation

Sallie Miles (Smith) -7/8/1894

Hugh Smith-6/16/1891

The Fourth Generation

Minnie Smith (Everett)-11/4/1914

Charles P. Everett, III-7/12/1912

The Fifth Generation

Charles P. Everett, IV-4/10/1947

Alfredia Y. Brown (Everett)-3/6/1945

The Brown's Family Branch

First Generation

Douglas Brown-1853-1921   Julia Ann White (Brown) 1862-1929

Hope Hull, Alabama   Montgomery County, Alabama

Children:

Anna B.

Linnie B.

Arthur

Mattie B.

Lottie

Lillian

Joseph-1896

Julia Mae

Oscar

Second Generation

Joseph Brown-2/15/1896   Betty Hurst (Brown) 2/15/1902

Hope Hull, Alabama

Third Generation

Ophelia Brown 12/30/1923	Charles Young
Joseph Brown, Jr. 9/9/1925	Florence
Fred Douglas Brown 10/31/1927	Lillie
Julia Mae Brown 11/1/1929	Leon L. H. Hamilton
James Clark Brown 10/7/1931	Mary
Betty Marie Brown 11/1/1933	John Robinson
Gladys Jean Brown 3/22/1941	Timothy Nelson
Alfredia Yvonne Brown 3/6/1945	Charles P. Everett, IV 4/10/1947

The Benson's Family Branch

Slave Owners   Dave Murrell-1833 and Mandy Murrell-1836

Virginia

First Generation

Charles Benson (Mulatto)-circa 1824   Sophie (Murrell) Benson-1833

Virginia   (parents unknown)

Virginia

He was a Union soldier in the Civil War – 1863 – 1865.

Children:

Monroe – circa 1855

Elizabeth Betsy or Betty - circa 1862

Vinnie or Viny -1865

Virginia-1869

Charles-1871

Elvey or Alvy-1873

Thomas or Tommie-1877

Second Generation

Elisabeth Betsy Benson (Hurst) circa 1862 - 1956   Clarke Hurst-1864

Marriage - 1886

Hope Hull, Alabama

Children:

Sophia-1887

David-1889

Susan-1890

James-1892

Georgia-1894

Mary-1897

Charles-1900

Betty-1902

Theodore-1905

Third Generation

Betty Hurst (Brown) 2/15/1902   Joseph Brown-2/15/1896
Hope Hull, Alabama

Fourth Generation

Alfredia Brown (Everett)   Charles P. Everett, IV-4/10/47

The Hurst's Family Branch

Slave Owners – A. W. Hurst 1822 North Carolina and David Hurst 1857

First Generation

Lewis Hurst   Leddie Hurst
BP Unknown
Children:
Henry
Clarke - 1864

Second Generation

Clarke Hurst- 1864-1942   Betsy Benson (Hurst) – circa 1862-1956
Union Academy, Alabama
Children:
Sophia- 1887
David – 1889
Susan – 1890
James 1892
Georgia – 1894
Mary – 1897
Charles – 1899
Betty – 1902
Theodore – 1905

Third Generation
Married 1/7/1923

Betty Hurst (Brown) – 1902-1976   Joseph Brown – 1896-1968
Hope Hull, Alabama   Hope Hull, Alabama
Children:
Ophelia 12/30/1923
Joseph 9/9/1925
Frederick Douglas 10/31/1927
Julia 11/9/1929
James 10/7/1931
Betty 11/1/1933
Gladys 3/22/1941
Alfredia- 3/6/ 1945

Fourth Generation

Alfredia Yvonne Brown (Everett) 3/6/45   Charles P. Everett, IV- 4/10/47
Hope Hull, Alabama   Montgomery, Alabama

BIBLIOGRAPHY

Everett, Yolanda, <u>Peter and the Boycott</u>, (Bloomington: AuthorHouse Publishing Co., (2014).

Haley, Alex, <u>Roots</u>, (Garden City: Doubleday, (1976).

Sprinthall, Norman A., Richard C. Sprinthall, and Sharon N. Oja, <u>Educational Psychology a Developmental Approach</u>, (New York: McGraw-Hill, Inc. (1994).

Special Sources

Alabama Corporates Company Profiles: AlabamaCorporates.com, 2013.

Caswell County Will Books 1843-1868.

Emancipation Proclamation, January 1, 1863; Presidential Proclamations, 1791-1991; Record Group 11; General Records of the United States Government; National Archives.

Everett, Minnie S. (1956, August) <u>Negro Life and History in the Social Studies Courses in the Elementary Schools of Autauga County, Alabama 1955 – 1956</u>. Unpublished.

Minutes of the Autauga County Board of Education for August 5, 1940, and March 11, 1942.

Photograph of the Graduating Class of Hampton Institute,1895. (Photograph Courtesy of Hampton University).

Photograph of the First U. S. Colored Infantry, Mathew Brady – Photographer (Courtesy Library of Congress)

Photograph of Veterans at the Southern Branch of the National Home for Disabled Veterans in Hampton, Virginia (Courtesy of the Library of Congress).

Photograph of Antioch Baptist Church (Circa 1896) (Courtesy Georgia Washington Junior High School)

Photograph of People's Village School Building (Circa 1896). (Courtesy Georgia Washington Junior Hight School).

Jackson, Keith. The Montgomery Monitor, "Teaching Has Been Wonderful for Us.", June 23 1976.

Order - November Term 1858; Reports of Cases in Equity, Supreme Court of North Carolina, December 1859-August 1860.

The Fifth Annual Report of the Principal of the People's Village School; Mount Meigs Village, Montgomery Co., Alabama; 1897. (Courtesy of Hampton University).

The Tuskegee Institute Choir. (Courtesy WSFA Television).

The Tuskegee Messenger, Vol. IX No. 6, "Commencement at Tuskegee Institute: "Big Day" in Macon County Tuskegee Institute, May 1933.

Tuskeana, Tuskegee Institute, 1965.

Wikipedia. "Jeanes Foundation", (June 13, 2020, at 5:34 (UTC). Retrieved from URL.

Printed in the United States
by Baker & Taylor Publisher Services